All The Presidents is dedicated to Nick Meglin, wonderful teacher, wonderful editor, wonderful friend.

FANTAGRAPHICS BOOKS INC.
7563 Lake City Way NE
Seattle, Washington, 98115
www.fantagraphics.com

Editor and Associate Publisher: Eric Reynolds
Book Design: Keeli McCarthy
Editorial assistance: Kevin Dougherty
Production: Paul Baresh
"Drawn to Presidents" lettering: Phil Felix
Proofreading: Kate Thomas
Publisher: Gary Groth

ISBN 978-1-68396-259-5
Library of Congress Control Number 2019933465

First printing: October 2019
Printed in China

ALL THE
PRESIDENTS

DREW FRIEDMAN

FOREWORD BY KURT ANDERSEN

FANTAGRAPHICS BOOKS

ALL THE PRESIDENTS

1	GEORGE WASHINGTON		23	BENJAMIN HARRISON
2	JOHN ADAMS		25	WILLIAM MCKINLEY
3	THOMAS JEFFERSON		26	THEODORE ROOSEVELT
4	JAMES MADISON		27	WILLIAM HOWARD TAFT
5	JAMES MONROE		28	WOODROW WILSON
6	JOHN QUINCY ADAMS		29	WARREN G. HARDING
7	ANDREW JACKSON		30	CALVIN COOLIDGE
8	MARTIN VAN BUREN		31	HERBERT C. HOOVER
9	WILLIAM HENRY HARRISON		32	FRANKLIN D. ROOSEVELT
10	JOHN TYLER		33	HARRY S. TRUMAN
11	JAMES K. POLK		34	DWIGHT D. EISENHOWER
12	ZACHARY TAYLOR		35	JOHN F. KENNEDY
13	MILLARD FILLMORE		36	LYNDON B. JOHNSON
14	FRANKLIN PIERCE		37	RICHARD M. NIXON
15	JAMES BUCHANAN		38	GERALD R. FORD
16	ABRAHAM LINCOLN		39	JAMES (JIMMY) E. CARTER
17	ANDREW JOHNSON		40	RONALD W. REAGAN
18	ULYSSES S. GRANT		41	GEORGE H. W. BUSH
19	RUTHERFORD B. HAYES		42	WILLIAM (BILL) J. CLINTON
20	JAMES A. GARFIELD		43	GEORGE W. BUSH
21	CHESTER A. ARTHUR		44	BARACK OBAMA
22 & 24	GROVER CLEVELAND		45	DONALD J. TRUMP

FOREWORD

I just realized: I've been a Drew Friedman fan for most of my life.

In 1986, Graydon Carter and I were creating *Spy* magazine. It was a satirical monthly, a hybrid of journalism and humor whose founding slogan was "Smart Fun Funny Fearless." We were both illustration enthusiasts, but in order to convey the fact-based fundamentals of our peculiar new magazine, we decided the covers needed to be photographs, not drawings or paintings, mostly with celebrity collaborators posing. (By the way, Photoshop didn't exist. Nor did the Internet, as we know it. Although there were aeroplanes and moving pictures, I'm pretty certain.)

Early on we came up with an idea for an illustrated monthly feature that would step beyond the strictly journalistic into topical speculative fiction. Each would be an artist's rendition of a plausible moment in the life of some newsworthy person who deserved ridicule, a drawing-as-photograph with a deadpan, newspho-to-style caption. We had a name, "Private Lives of Public Figures," but we needed a kindred-spirit illustrator to execute our ideas.

We discovered Drew. A book of his work, *Any Similarity to Persons Living or Dead is Purely Coincidental* (Fantagraphics Books, 1986), had just been published. We loved everything about it — the title, the singular style, the breathtaking skill, the insanely labor intensive stippling, the fact that one of his portraits was of the TV quiz show host, Wink Martindale.

Drew's sensibility overlapped nicely with our sensibilities. In the beginning, when we were paying him $175 a pop, *Spy* had a subtitle: "The New York Month-ly." His gleefully and accurately unkind pictures seemed to us quintessentially New York, a cruddy and glamorous and weird black-and-white *Sweet Smell of Success* and Diane Arbus New York, a style perfect for depicting the grifters and jerks of the new celebrity tragicomedy erupting in the go-go 1980s. As Drew himself re-cently described his approach to portraiture, his faces tend to feature "warts, pim-ples, wrinkles, flop-sweat, jowls, boils, rosacea, nose hairs, ear hairs, drool, baggy eyes, gin blossoms, moles, liver spots, neck waddles… double chins, triple chins, blotches, scars, lumps, zits, five o'clock shadows… bald heads, nodules, freckles, protuberances, welts, carbuncles," etcetera, ad infinitum.

Over the next six years, Drew produced all 65 monthly installments of "Pri-vate Lives of Public Figures," among them his first drawings ever of three U.S. presidents: Ronald Reagan, George H.W. Bush, and Bill Clinton. As well as two starring a future president, a recurring *Spy* character on whom we tried out vari-ous epithets — "Queens-born casino operator," "well-fed condo hustler" — before landing on the one that stuck, "short-fingered vulgarian Donald Trump."

The pictures Drew Friedman made for this book are all instantly recognizable as his work, but the grotesquerie has been dialed back. Maybe because our bril-liantly vicious young portraitist works in more registers now, or has mellowed with age. Or maybe because what would be the point of showing Chester Allan Arthur's warts, ear hairs, liver spots, and carbuncles? The sheer virtuosity, however, remains as astounding as ever. And sometimes achieves the sublime. In particular, I keep returning to the portraits of Woodrow Wilson and Barack Obama, and not just because I voted for one of them twice. Both are unsentimentally beautiful and revealing and true.

To my eye, only one of these 44 pictures is distinctly unflattering, but not because Drew let his old warts-and-all-and-*more*-warts viciousness run wild. In fact, any ordinary photograph of President Trump — ridiculous golden hair, ridiculous golden skin, jowls and chins and raccoon eyes — is pretty unflattering. What *this* revealing and true portrait renders unmistakably is the misery and wretchedness of the man within. The first time I saw it I shuddered, which is quite a thing for a drawing to do.

— Kurt Andersen

Kurt Andersen is the author and host of public radio's Studio 360.

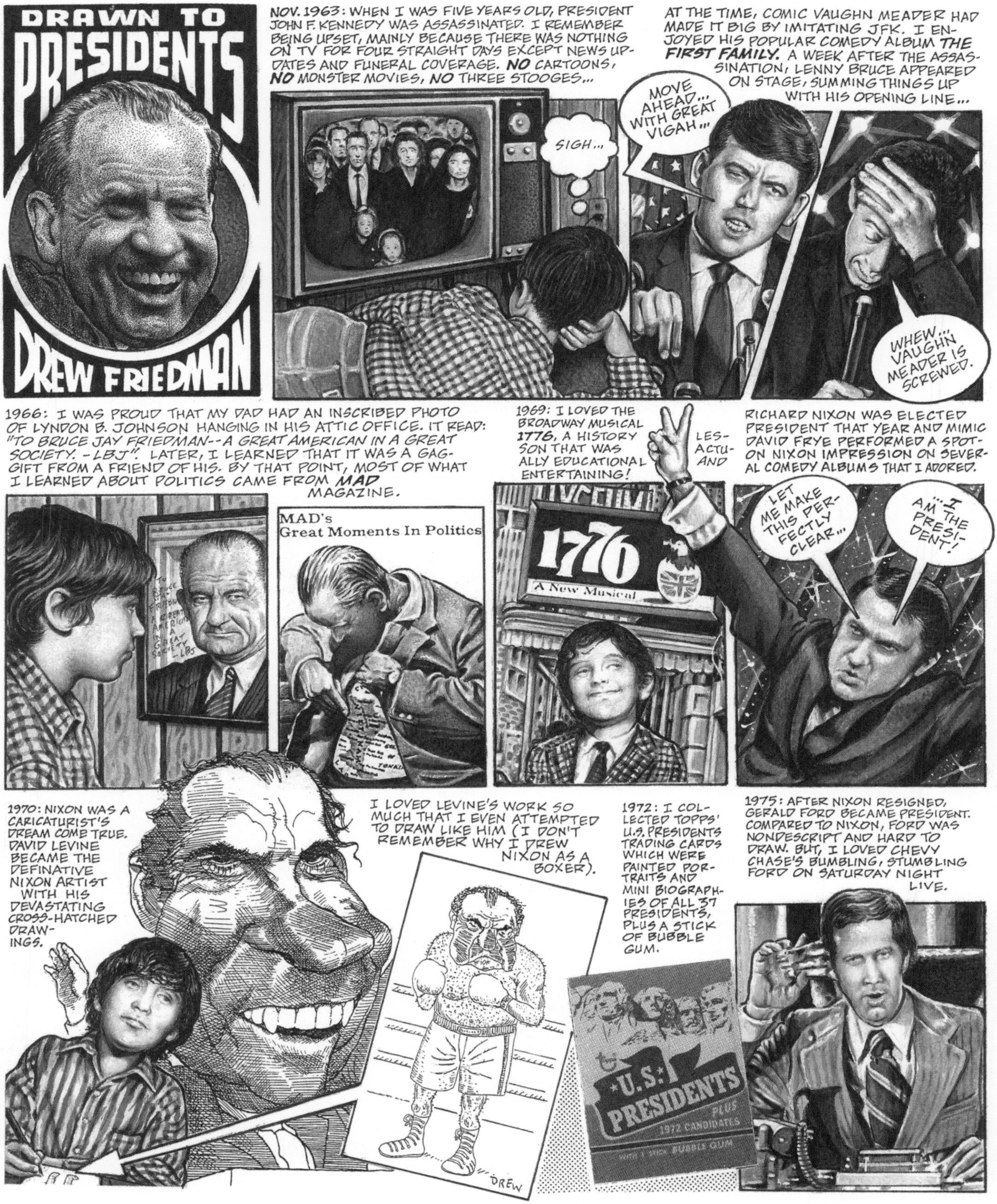

DRAWN TO
PRESIDENTS
DREW FRIEDMAN
NOV. 1963: WHEN I WAS FIVE YEARS OLD, PRESIDENT JOHN F. KENNEDY WAS ASSASSINATED. I REMEMBER BEING UPSET, MAINLY BECAUSE THERE WAS NOTHING ON TV FOR FOUR STRAIGHT DAYS EXCEPT NEWS UPDATES AND FUNERAL COVERAGE. NO CARTOONS, NO MONSTER MOVIES, NO THREE STOOGES...
SIGH...
AT THE TIME, COMIC VAUGHN MEADER HAD MADE IT BIG BY IMITATING JFK. I ENJOYED HIS POPULAR COMEDY ALBUM THE FIRST FAMILY. A WEEK AFTER THE ASSASSINATION, LENNY BRUCE APPEARED ON STAGE, SUMMING THINGS UP WITH HIS OPENING LINE...
MOVE AHEAD... WITH GREAT VIGAH...
WHEW... VAUGHN MEADER IS SCREWED.
1966: I WAS PROUD THAT MY DAD HAD AN INSCRIBED PHOTO OF LYNDON B. JOHNSON HANGING IN HIS ATTIC OFFICE. IT READ: "TO BRUCE JAY FRIEDMAN--A GREAT AMERICAN IN A GREAT SOCIETY. -LBJ". LATER, I LEARNED THAT IT WAS A GAG-GIFT FROM A FRIEND OF HIS. BY THAT POINT, MOST OF WHAT I LEARNED ABOUT POLITICS CAME FROM MAD MAGAZINE.
MAD's Great Moments In Politics
1969: I LOVED THE BROADWAY MUSICAL 1776, A HISTORY LESSON THAT WAS ACTUALLY EDUCATIONAL AND ENTERTAINING!
1776
A New Musical
RICHARD NIXON WAS ELECTED PRESIDENT THAT YEAR AND MIMIC DAVID FRYE PERFORMED A SPOT-ON NIXON IMPRESSION ON SEVERAL COMEDY ALBUMS THAT I ADORED.
LET ME MAKE THIS PERFECTLY CLEAR...
...I AM THE PRESIDENT!
1970: NIXON WAS A CARICATURIST'S DREAM COME TRUE. DAVID LEVINE BECAME THE DEFINATIVE NIXON ARTIST WITH HIS DEVASTATING CROSS-HATCHED DRAWINGS.
I LOVED LEVINE'S WORK SO MUCH THAT I EVEN ATTEMPTED TO DRAW LIKE HIM (I DON'T REMEMBER WHY I DREW NIXON AS A BOXER).
DREW
1972: I COLLECTED TOPPS' U.S. PRESIDENTS TRADING CARDS WHICH WERE PAINTED PORTRAITS AND MINI BIOGRAPHIES OF ALL 37 PRESIDENTS, PLUS A STICK OF BUBBLE GUM.
U.S. PRESIDENTS
PLUS
1972 CANDIDATES
WITH 1 STICK BUBBLE GUM
1975: AFTER NIXON RESIGNED, GERALD FORD BECAME PRESIDENT. COMPARED TO NIXON, FORD WAS NONDESCRIPT AND HARD TO DRAW. BUT, I LOVED CHEVY CHASE'S BUMBLING, STUMBLING FORD ON SATURDAY NIGHT LIVE.

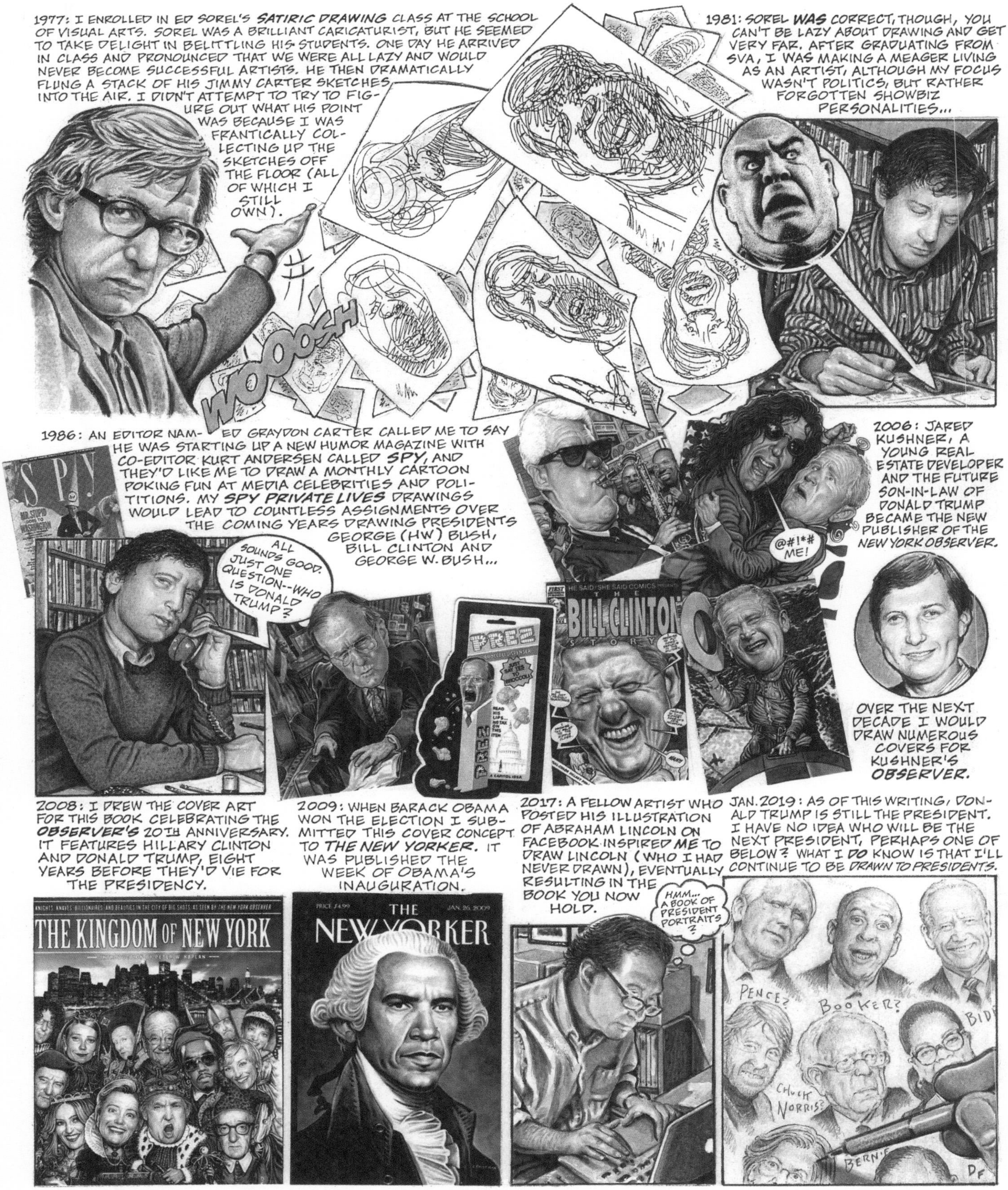
1977: I ENROLLED IN ED SOREL'S SATIRIC DRAWING CLASS AT THE SCHOOL OF VISUAL ARTS. SOREL WAS A BRILLIANT CARICATURIST, BUT HE SEEMED TO TAKE DELIGHT IN BELITTLING HIS STUDENTS. ONE DAY HE ARRIVED IN CLASS AND PRONOUNCED THAT WE WERE ALL LAZY AND WOULD NEVER BECOME SUCCESSFUL ARTISTS. HE THEN DRAMATICALLY FLUNG A STACK OF HIS JIMMY CARTER SKETCHES INTO THE AIR. I DIDN'T ATTEMPT TO TRY TO FIGURE OUT WHAT HIS POINT WAS BECAUSE I WAS FRANTICALLY COLLECTING UP THE SKETCHES OFF THE FLOOR (ALL OF WHICH I STILL OWN).
WOOOSH
1981: SOREL WAS CORRECT, THOUGH, YOU CAN'T BE LAZY ABOUT DRAWING AND GET VERY FAR. AFTER GRADUATING FROM SVA, I WAS MAKING A MEAGER LIVING AS AN ARTIST, ALTHOUGH MY FOCUS WASN'T POLITICS, BUT RATHER FORGOTTEN SHOWBIZ PERSONALITIES...
1986: AN EDITOR NAMED GRAYDON CARTER CALLED ME TO SAY HE WAS STARTING UP A NEW HUMOR MAGAZINE WITH CO-EDITOR KURT ANDERSEN CALLED SPY, AND THEY'D LIKE ME TO DRAW A MONTHLY CARTOON POKING FUN AT MEDIA CELEBRITIES AND POLITITIONS. MY SPY PRIVATE LIVES DRAWINGS WOULD LEAD TO COUNTLESS ASSIGNMENTS OVER THE COMING YEARS DRAWING PRESIDENTS GEORGE (HW) BUSH, BILL CLINTON AND GEORGE W. BUSH...
SPY
ALL SOUNDS GOOD. JUST ONE QUESTION--WHO IS DONALD TRUMP?
@#!*# ME!
HE SAID/SHE SAID COMICS
THE BILL CLINTON STORY
2006: JARED KUSHNER, A YOUNG REAL ESTATE DEVELOPER AND THE FUTURE SON-IN-LAW OF DONALD TRUMP BECAME THE NEW PUBLISHER OF THE NEW YORK OBSERVER.
OVER THE NEXT DECADE I WOULD DRAW NUMEROUS COVERS FOR KUSHNER'S OBSERVER.
2008: I DREW THE COVER ART FOR THIS BOOK CELEBRATING THE OBSERVER'S 20TH ANNIVERSARY. IT FEATURES HILLARY CLINTON AND DONALD TRUMP, EIGHT YEARS BEFORE THEY'D VIE FOR THE PRESIDENCY.
2009: WHEN BARACK OBAMA WON THE ELECTION I SUBMITTED THIS COVER CONCEPT TO THE NEW YORKER. IT WAS PUBLISHED THE WEEK OF OBAMA'S INAUGURATION.
2017: A FELLOW ARTIST WHO POSTED HIS ILLUSTRATION OF ABRAHAM LINCOLN ON FACEBOOK INSPIRED ME TO DRAW LINCOLN (WHO I HAD NEVER DRAWN), EVENTUALLY RESULTING IN THE BOOK YOU NOW HOLD.
JAN. 2019: AS OF THIS WRITING, DONALD TRUMP IS STILL THE PRESIDENT. I HAVE NO IDEA WHO WILL BE THE NEXT PRESIDENT, PERHAPS ONE OF BELOW? WHAT I DO KNOW IS THAT I'LL CONTINUE TO BE DRAWN TO PRESIDENTS.
KNIGHTS · KNAVES · BILLIONAIRES · AND BEAUTIES IN THE CITY OF BIG SHOTS, AS SEEN BY THE NEW YORK OBSERVER
THE KINGDOM OF NEW YORK
PRICE $4.99 THE NEW YORKER JAN. 26, 2009
HMM... A BOOK OF PRESIDENT PORTRAITS?
PENCE?
BOOKER?
BID
CHUCK NORRIS?
BERNIE
DF

ALL THE PRESIDENTS

GEORGE WASHINGTON

BORN
February 22, 1732
Westmoreland County, Virginia

DIED
December 14, 1799

PARTY
None

TERM
1789–1797

AGE AT INAUGURATION
57

FUN FACT
Refused to serve a third term.

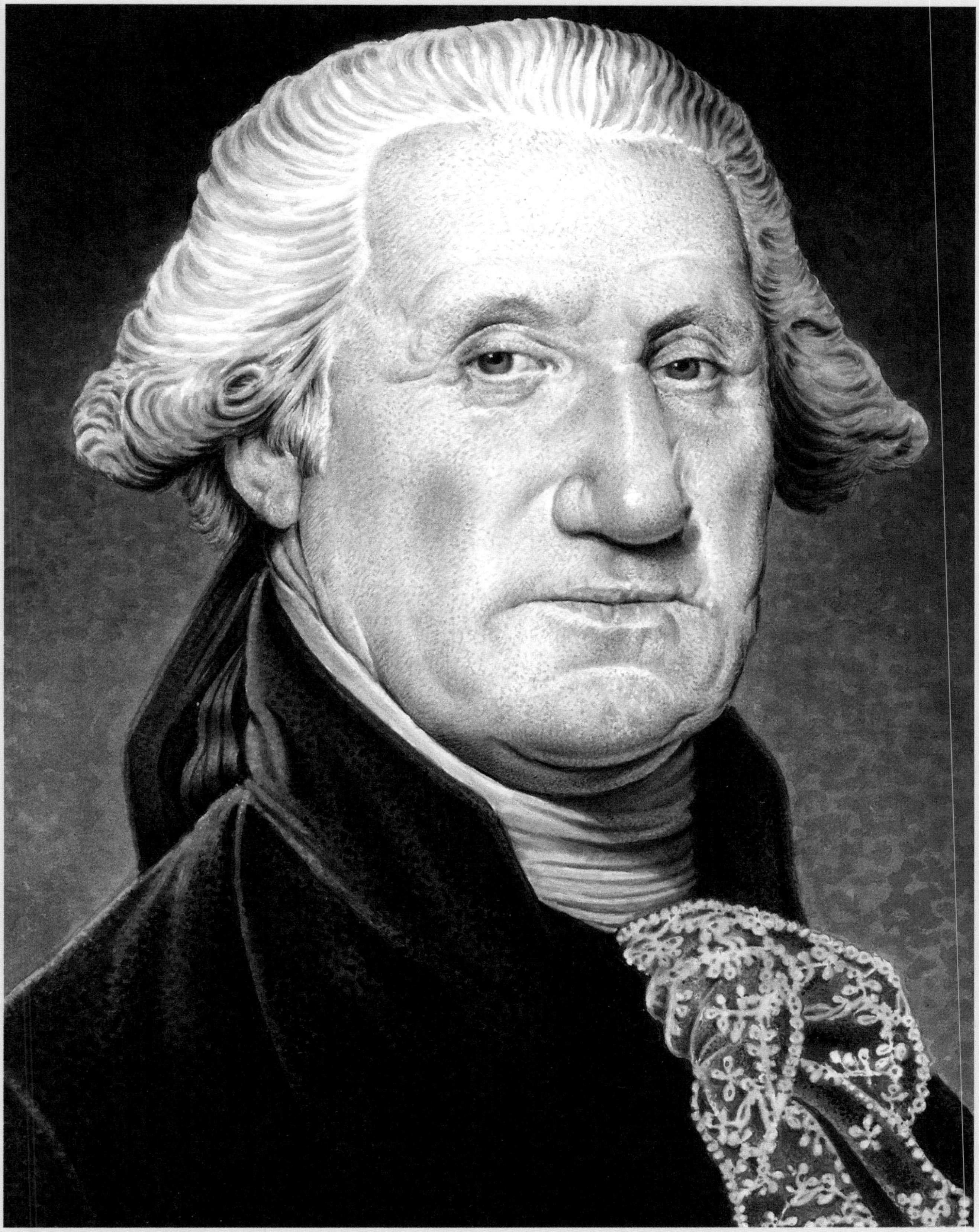

JOHN ADAMS

BORN
October 30, 1735
Braintree, Massachusetts

DIED
July 4, 1826

PARTY
Federalist

TERM
1797–1801

AGE AT INAUGURATION
61

FUN FACT
The first president to live in the White House.

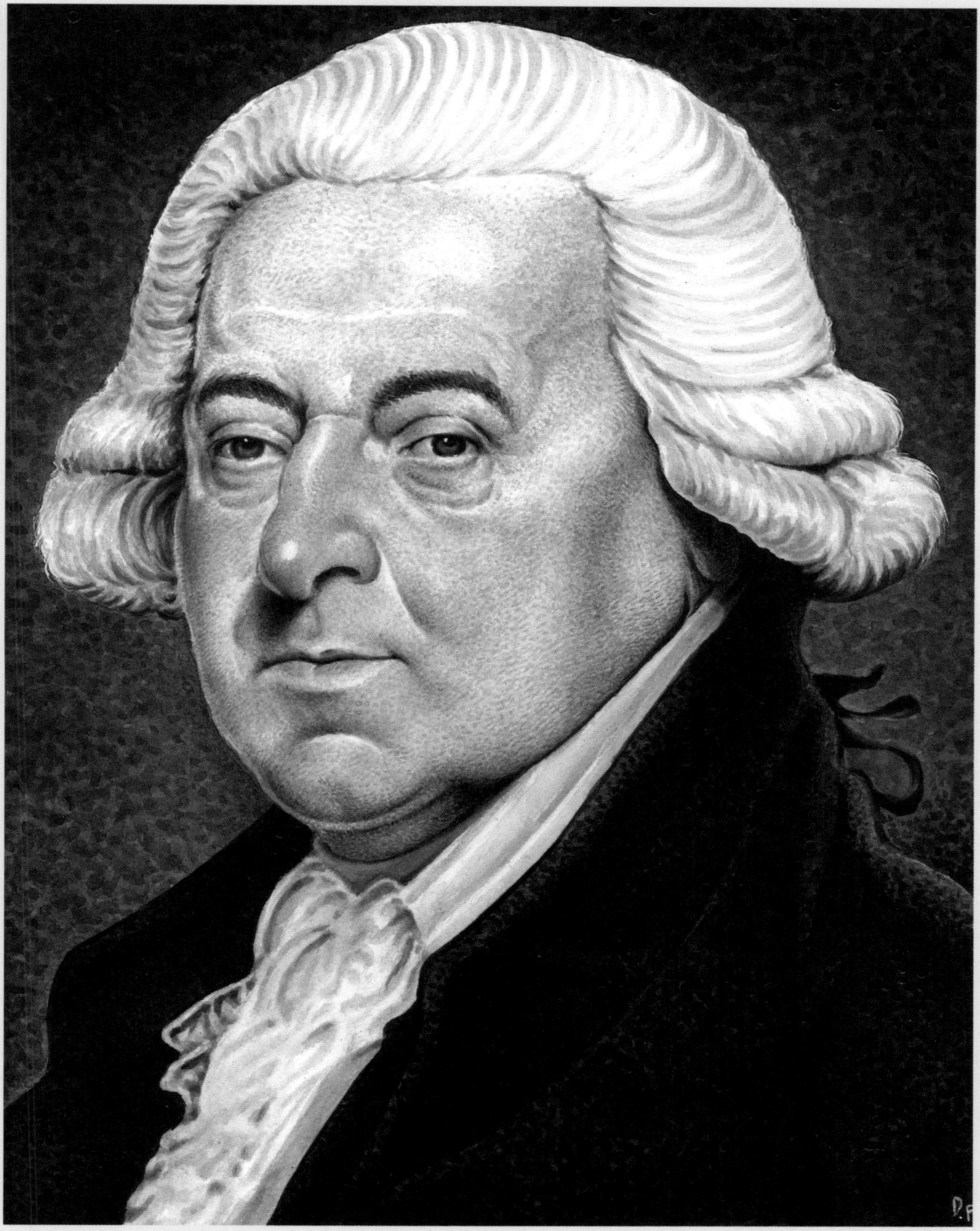

THOMAS JEFFERSON

BORN
April 13, 1743
Albemarle County, Virginia

DIED
July 4, 1826

PARTY
Democratic-Republican

TERM
1801–1809

AGE AT INAUGURATION
57

FUN FACT
Wrote the Declaration of Independence.

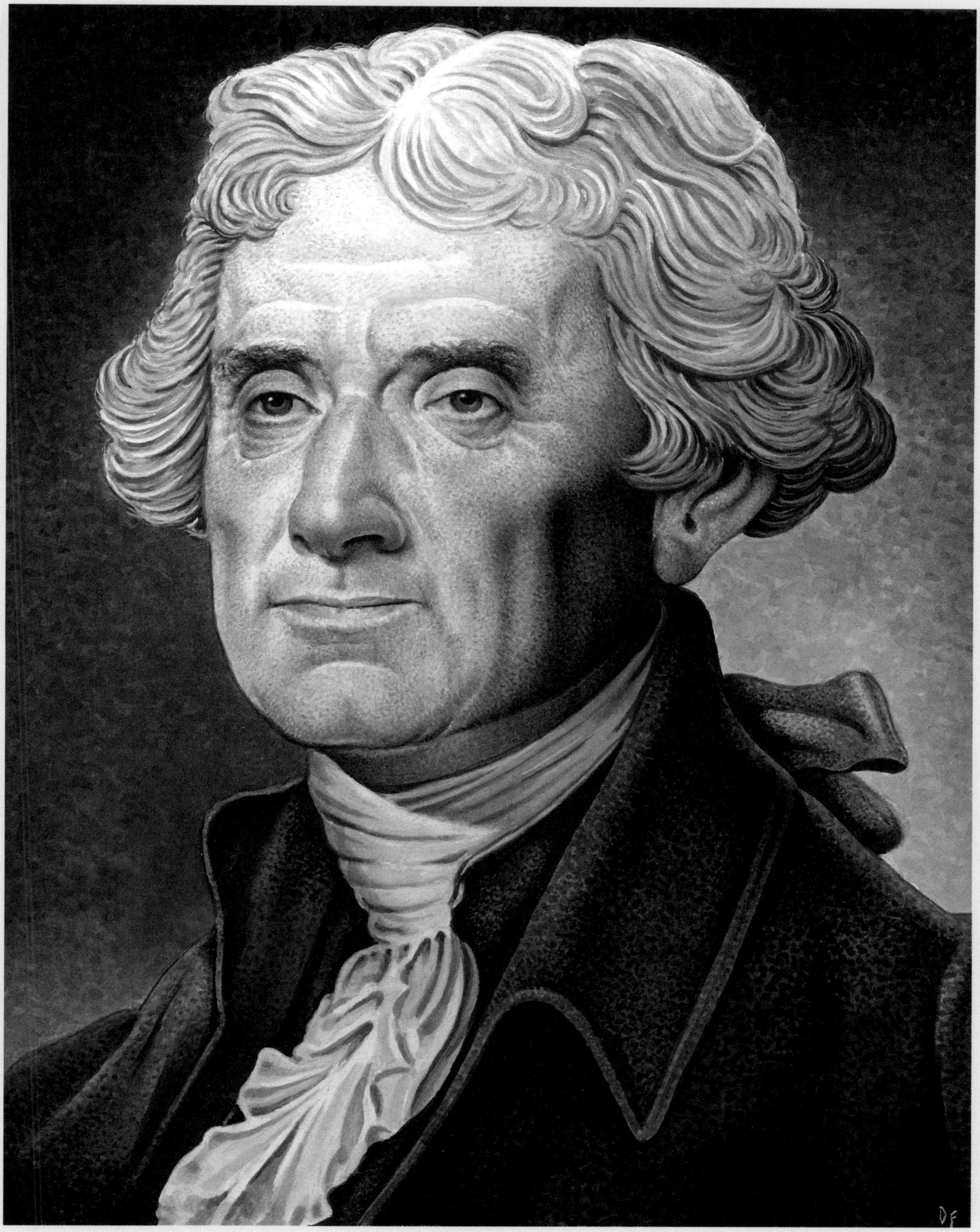
DF

JAMES MADISON, JR.

BORN
March 16, 1751
Port Conway, Virginia

DIED
June 28, 1836

PARTY
Democratic-Republican

TERM
1809–1817

AGE AT INAUGURATION
57

FUN FACT
Known as the father of the Constitution.

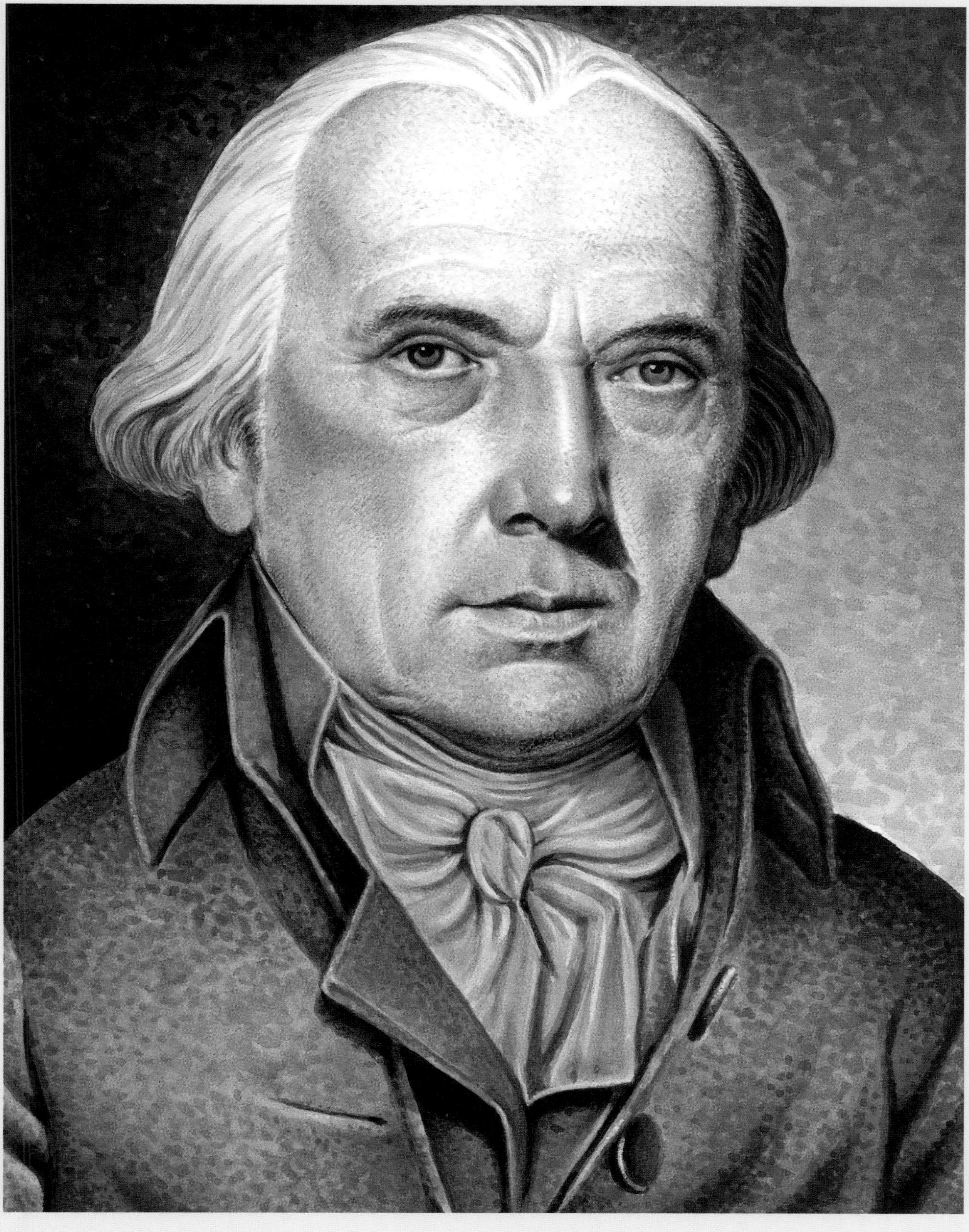

JAMES MONROE

BORN
April 28, 1758
Westmoreland County, Virginia

DIED
July 4, 1831

PARTY
Democratic-Republican

TERM
1817–1825

AGE AT INAUGURATION
58

FUN FACT
Monrovia, capital city of the West African
country Liberia, is named after Monroe.

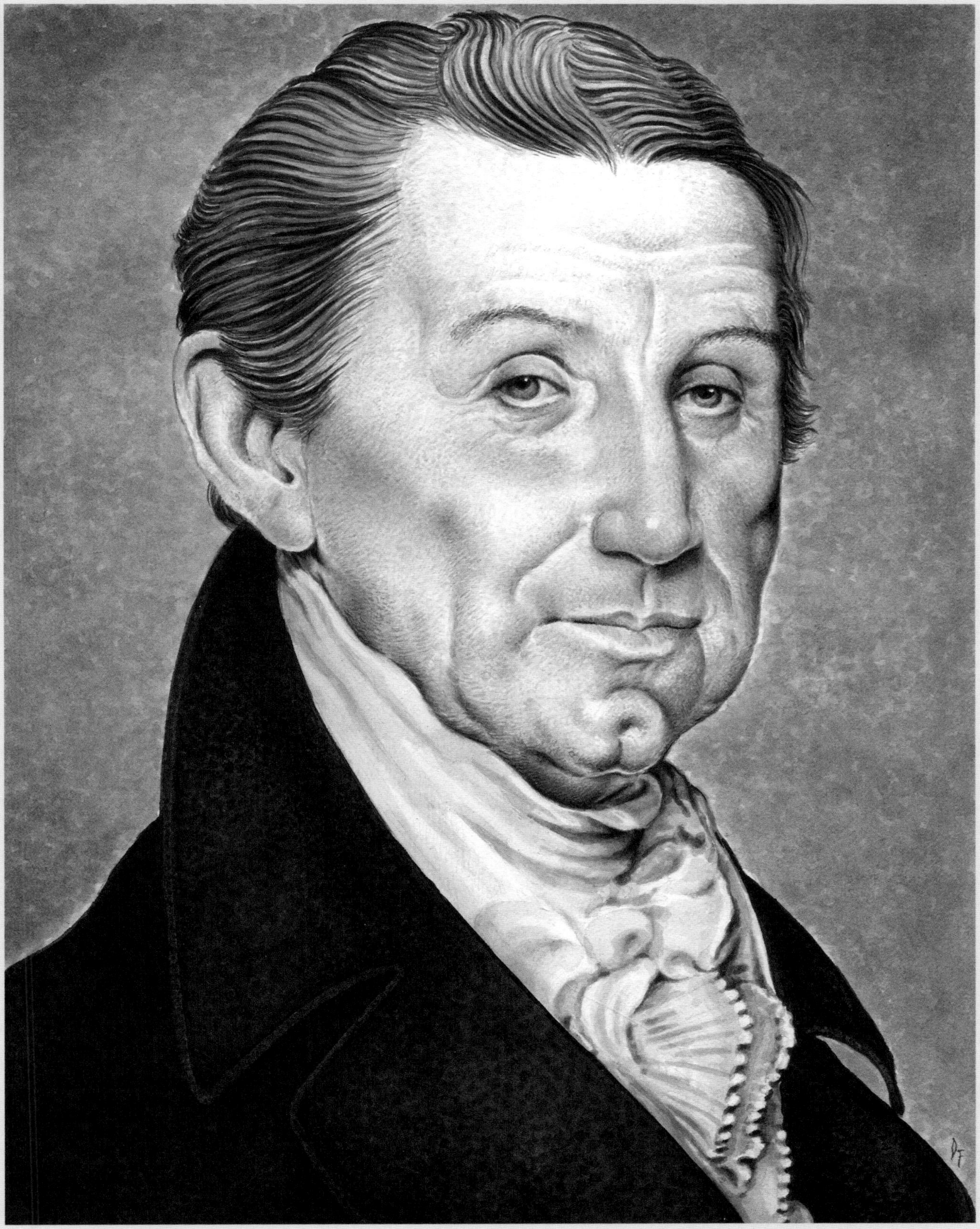

JOHN QUINCY ADAMS

BORN
July 11, 1767
Braintree, Massachusetts

DIED
February 23, 1848

PARTY
Democratic-Republican

TERM
1825–1829

AGE AT INAUGURATION
57

FUN FACT
Son of John Adams.

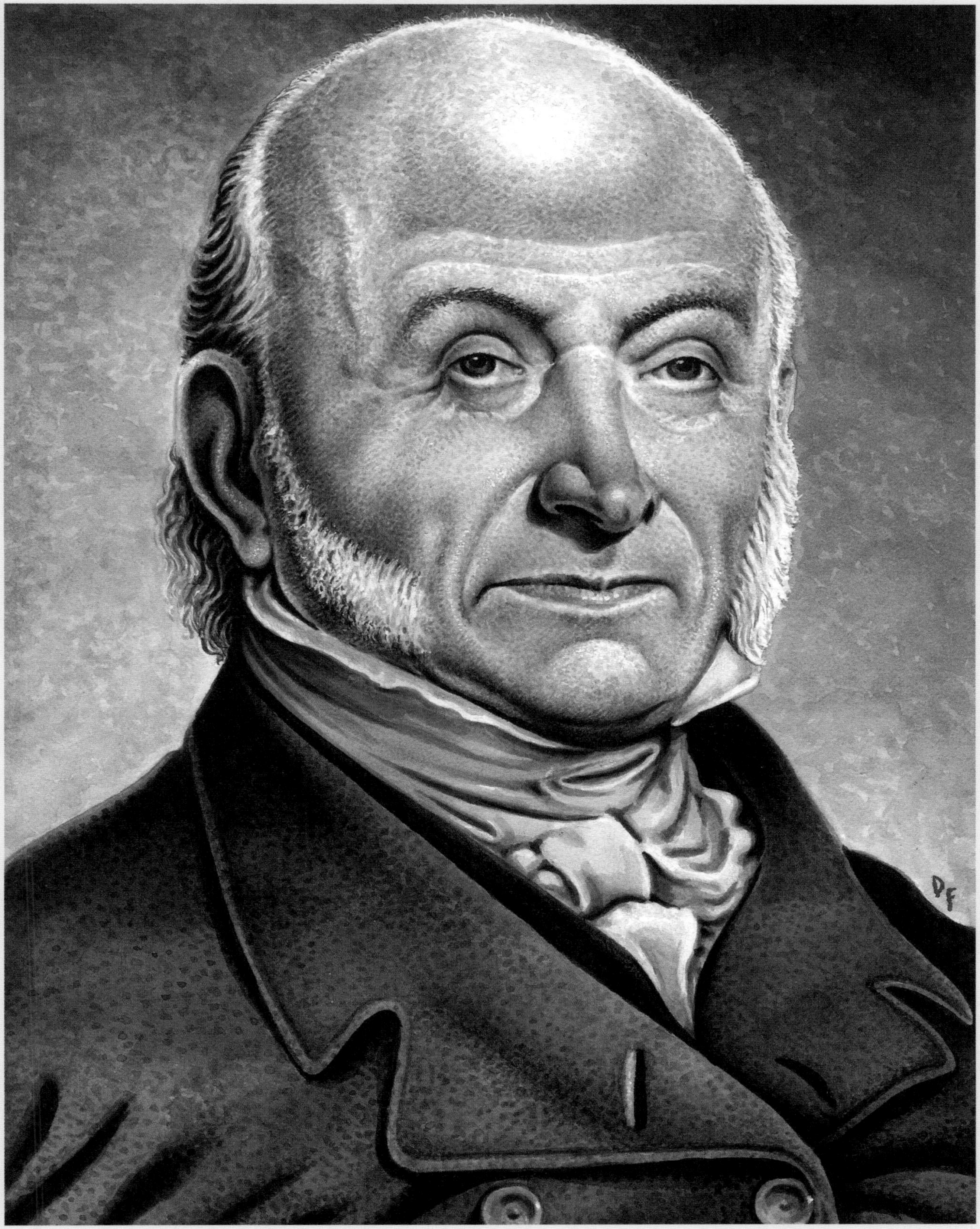
DF

ANDREW JACKSON

BORN
March 15, 1767
Waxhaw settlement, South Carolina

DIED
June 8, 1845

PARTY
Democratic

TERM
1829–1837

AGE AT INAUGURATION
61

FUN FACT
The first sitting president to ride on a train.

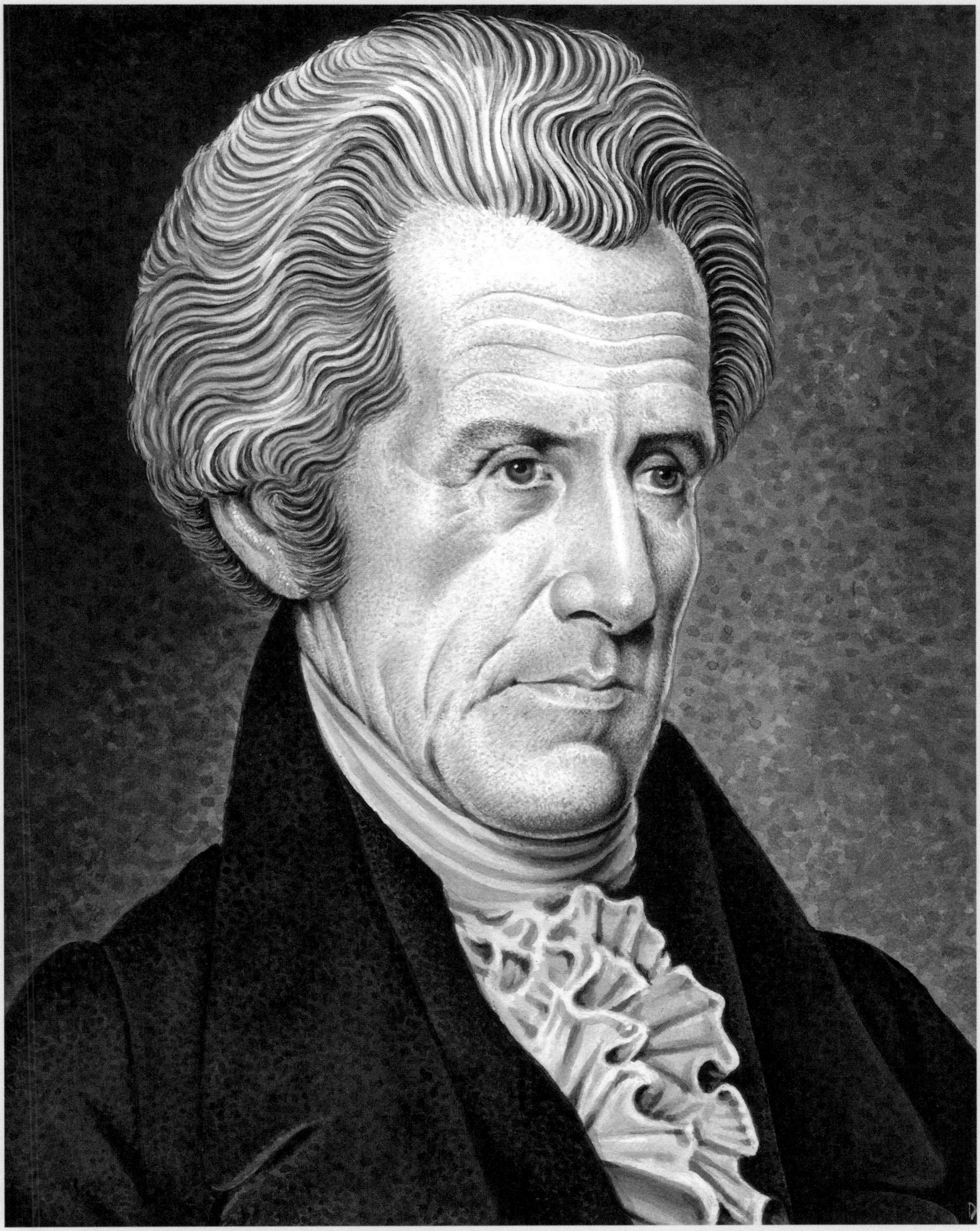

MARTIN VAN BUREN

BORN
December 5, 1782
Kinderhook, New York

DIED
July 24, 1862.

PARTY
Democrat

TERM
1837–1841

AGE AT INAUGURATION
54

FUN FACT
The first president who was born an American citizen.

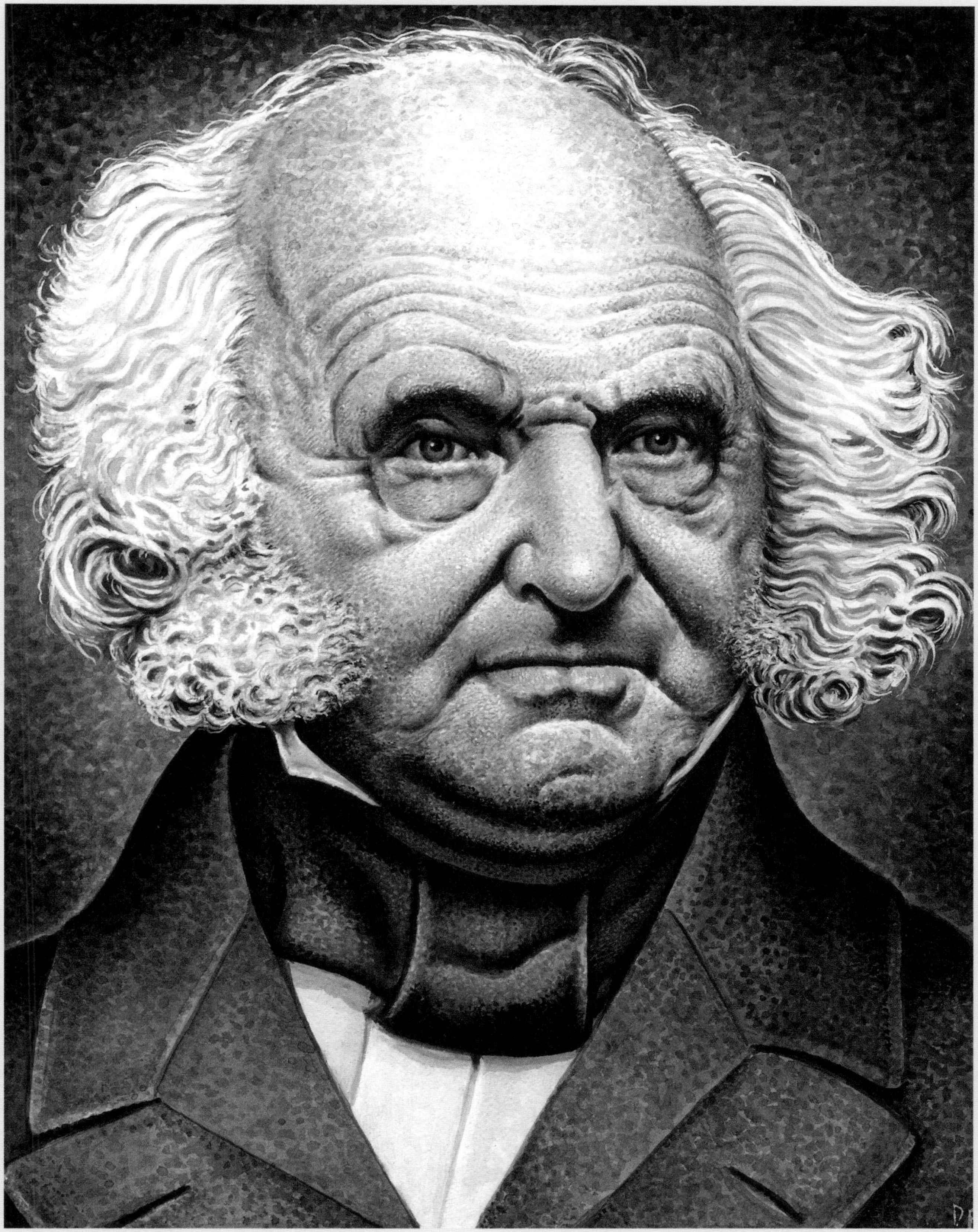

WILLIAM HENRY HARRISON

BORN
February 9, 1773
Berkeley, Virginia

DIED
April 4, 1841

PARTY
Whig

TERM
1841

AGE AT INAUGURATION
68

FUN FACT
Died a month after his inauguration.
He was the first president to die in office
and served the shortest term.

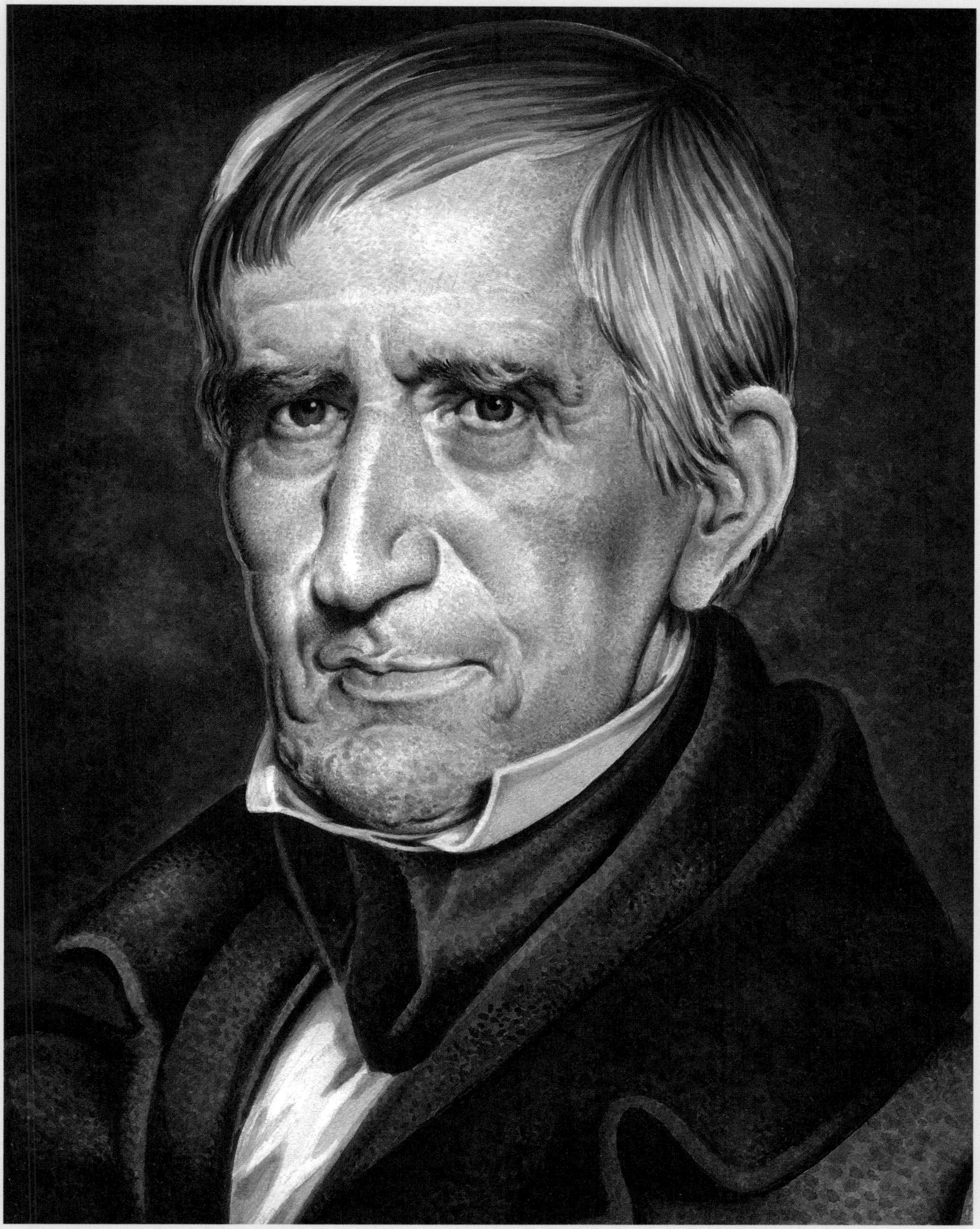

10

JOHN TYLER

BORN
March 29, 1790
Greenway, Virginia

DIED
January 18, 1862

PARTY
Whig

TERM
1841–1845

AGE AT INAUGURATION
51

FUN FACT
Fathered 15 children.

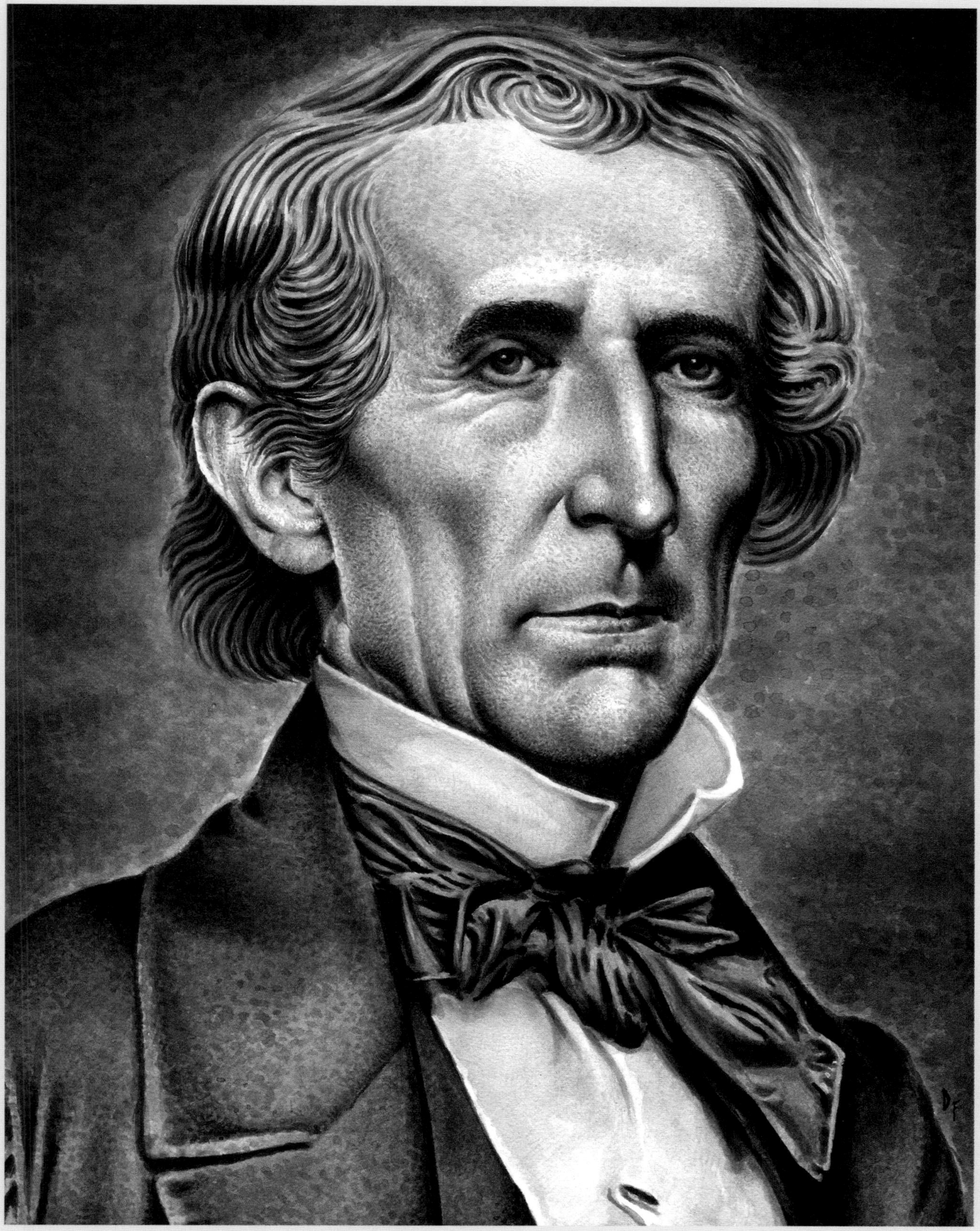

JAMES K. POLK

BORN
November 2, 1795
near Pineville, North Carolina

DIED
June 15, 1849

PARTY
Democratic

TERM
1845–1849

AGE AT INAUGURATION
49

FUN FACT
The first president to serve one self-imposed term.

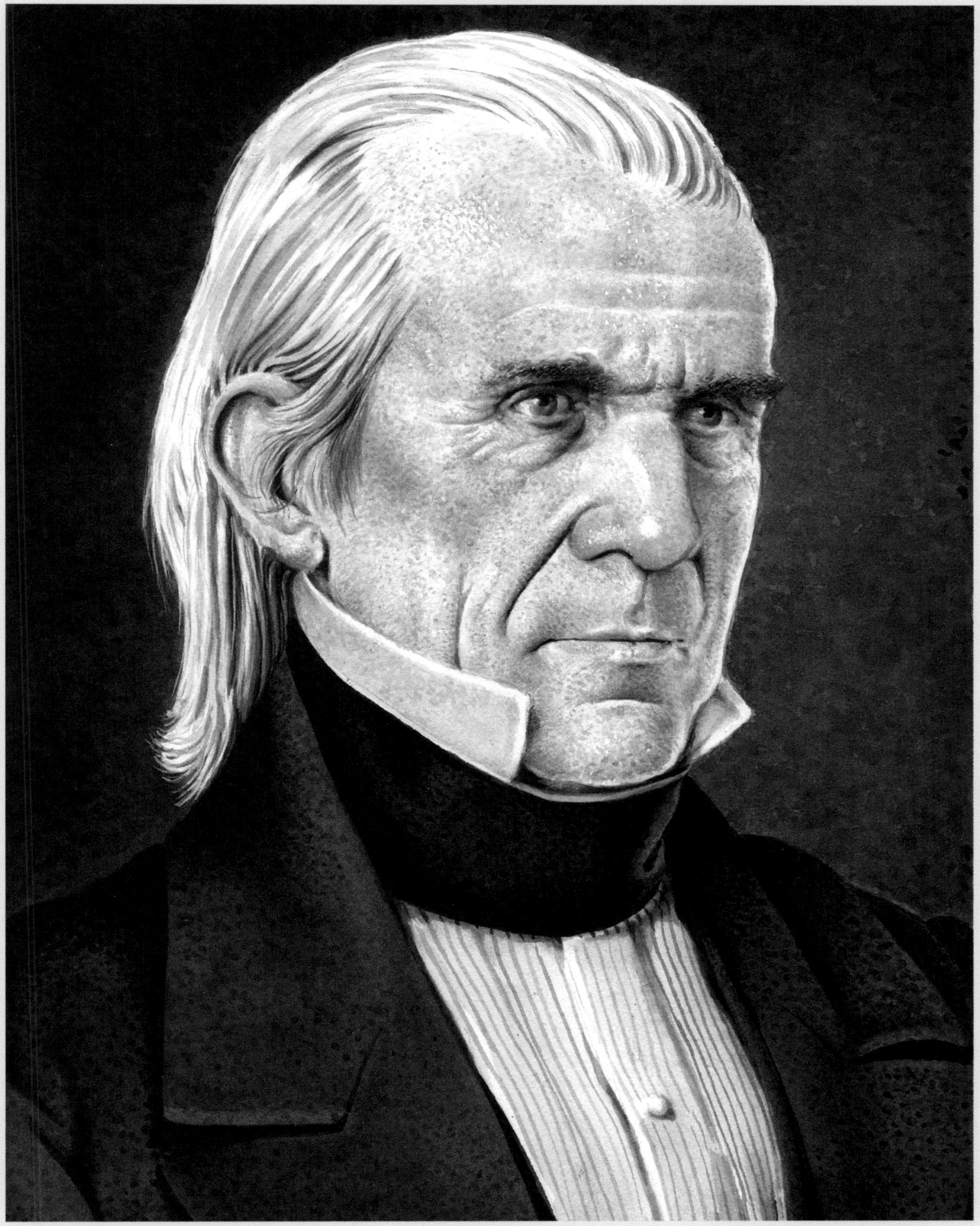

ZACHARY TAYLOR

BORN
November 24, 1784
Orange County, Virginia

DIED
July 9, 1850

PARTY
Whig

TERM
1849–1850

AGE AT INAUGURATION
64

FUN FACT
Died in office after consuming
a large quantity of cherries.

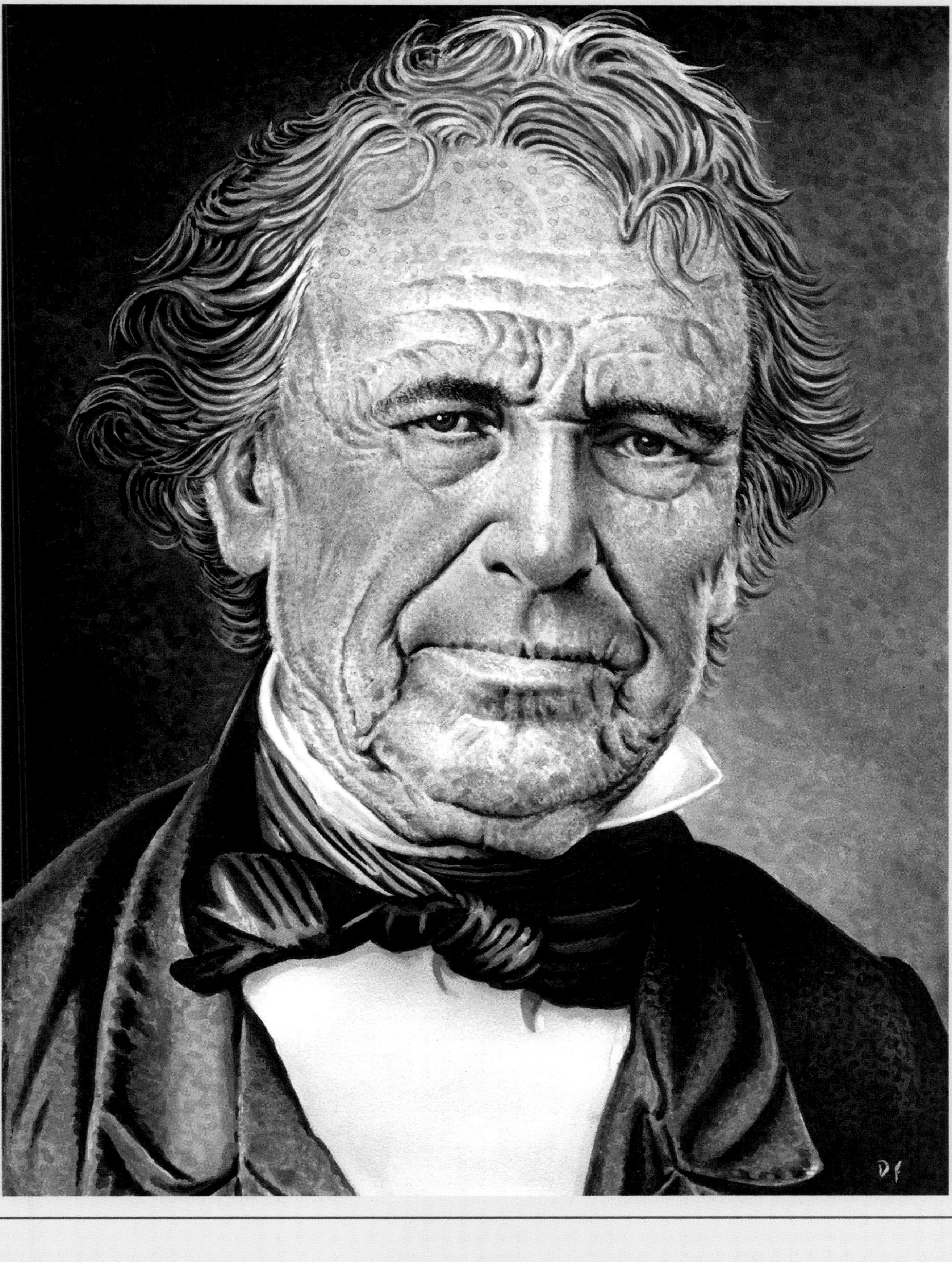

MILLARD FILLMORE

BORN
January 7, 1800
Locke, New York

DIED
March 8, 1874

PARTY
Whig

TERM
1850–1853

AGE AT INAUGURATION
50

FUN FACT
Did not have a vice-president.

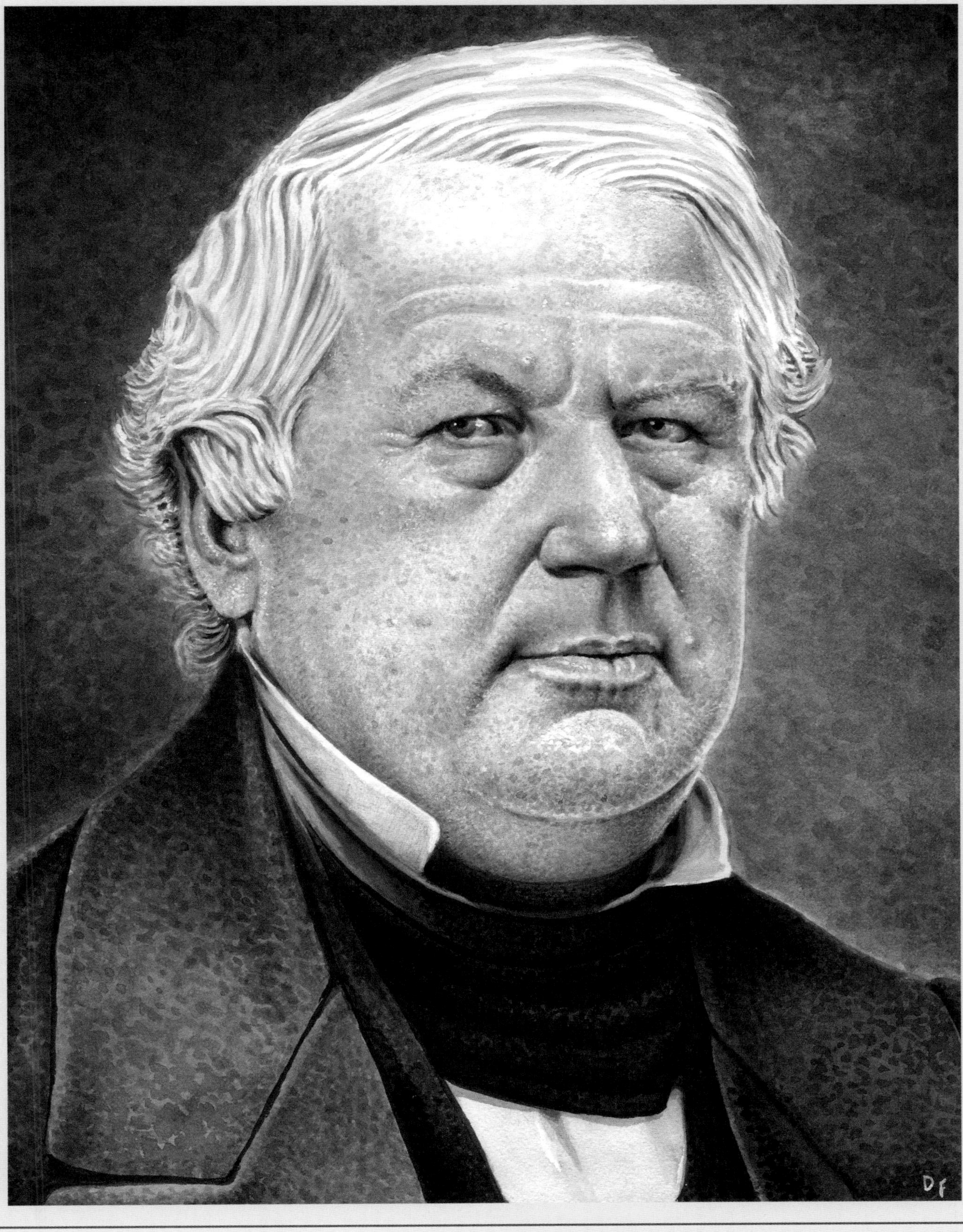
Df

FRANKLIN PIERCE

BORN
November 23, 1804
Hillsboro, New Hampshire

DIED
October 8, 1869

PARTY
Democratic

TERM
1853–1857

AGE AT INAUGURATION
48

FUN FACT
A heavy drinker; died of cirrhosis of the liver.

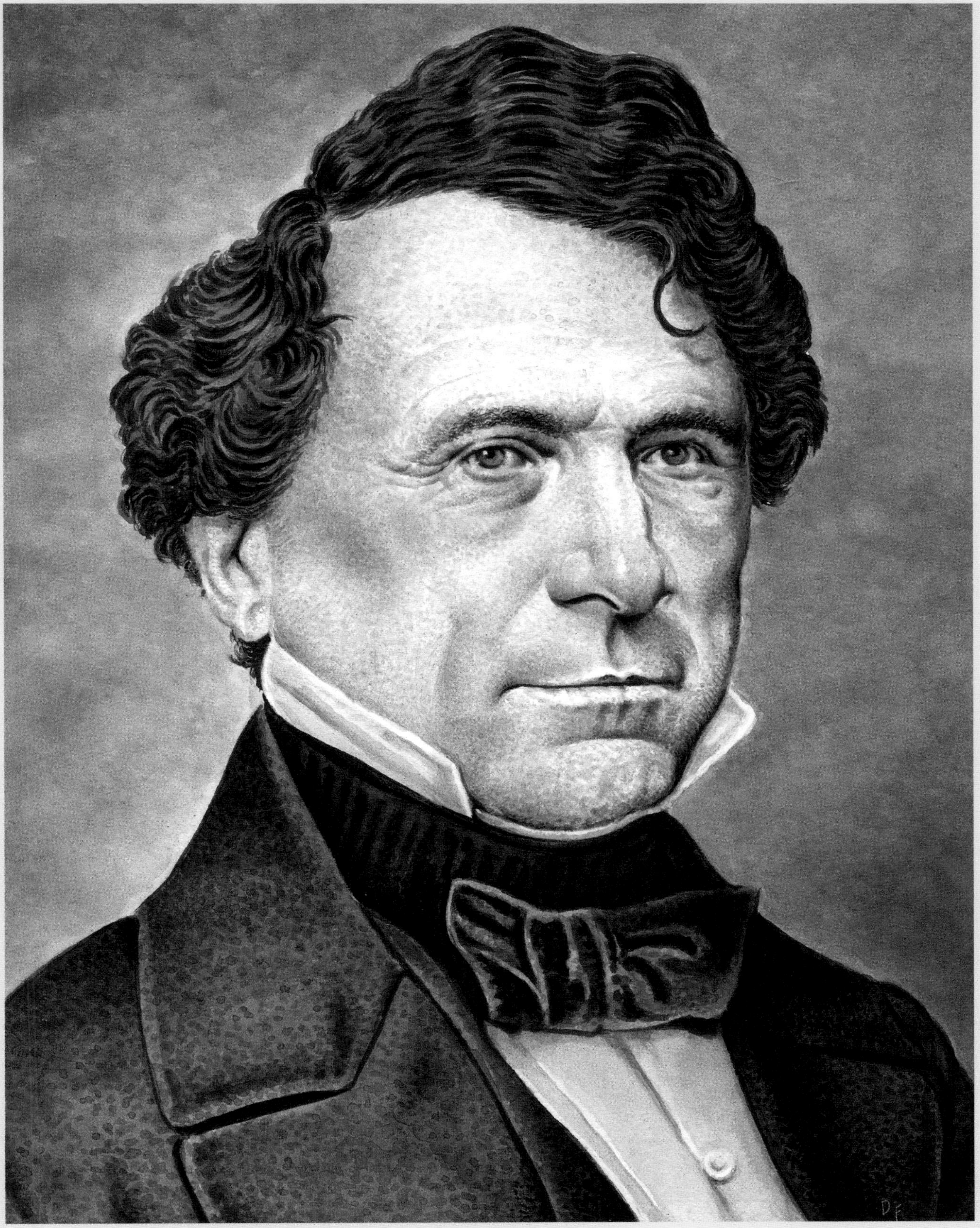

15

JAMES BUCHANAN

BORN
April 23, 1791
near Mercersburg, Pennsylvania

DIED
June 1, 1868

PARTY
Democratic

TERM
1857–1861

AGE AT INAUGURATION
65

FUN FACT
The only bachelor president.

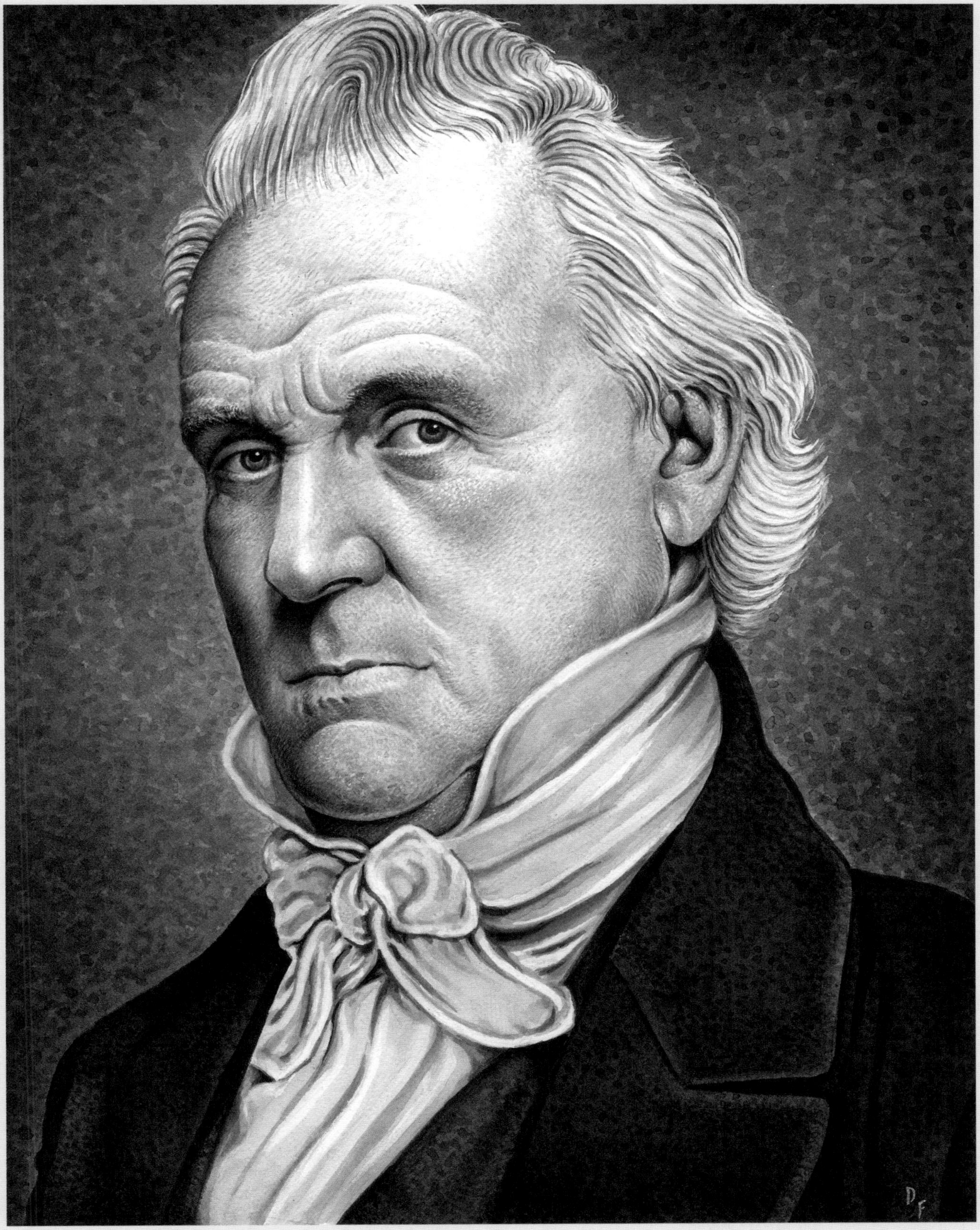

ABRAHAM LINCOLN

BORN
February 12, 1809
near Hodgenville, Kentucky

DIED
April 15, 1865

PARTY
Republican

TERM
1861–1865

AGE AT INAUGURATION
52

FUN FACT
Had a dog named Fido.

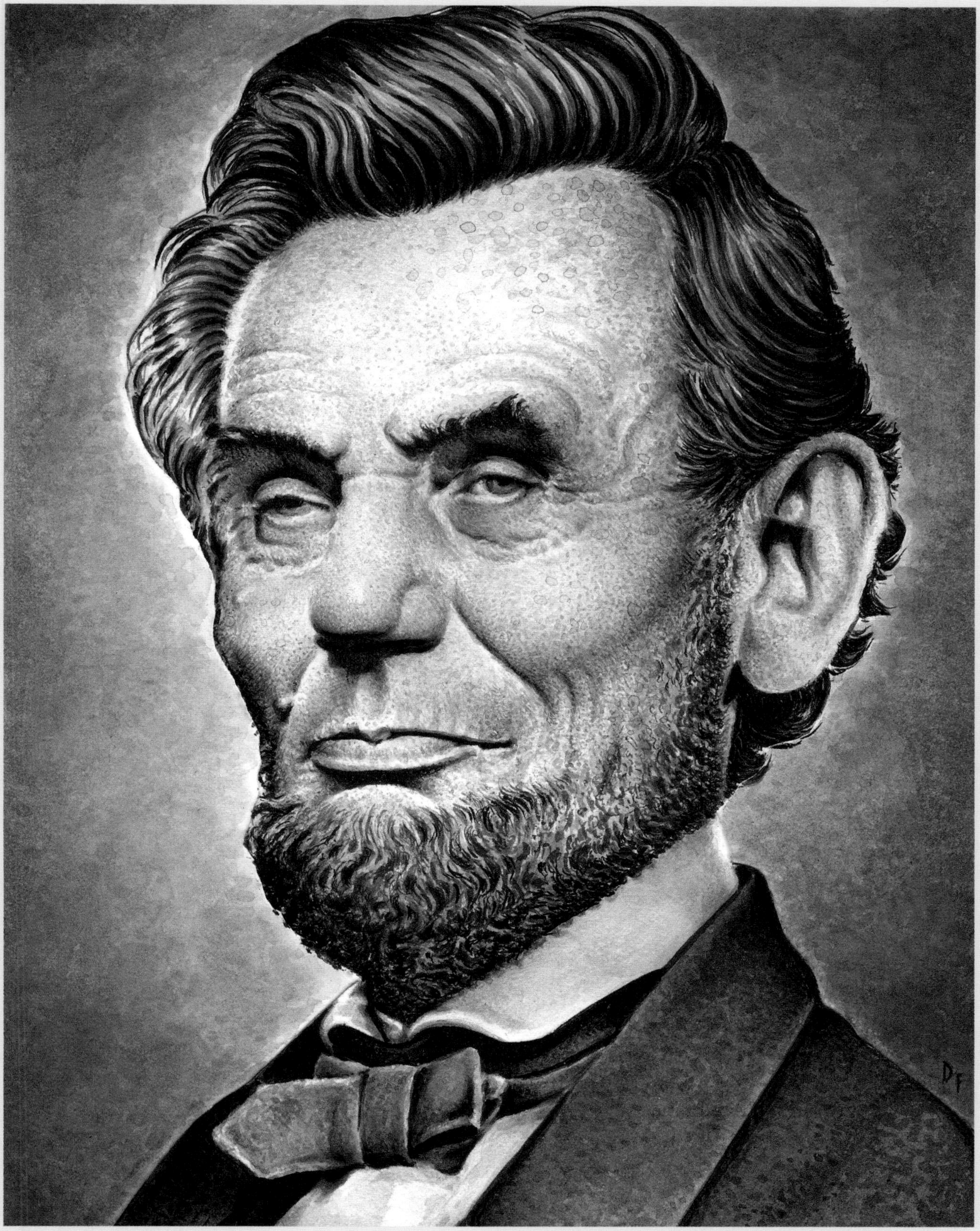

ANDREW JOHNSON

BORN
December 29, 1808
Raleigh, North Carolina

DIED
July 31, 1875

PARTY
National Union

TERM
1865–1869

AGE AT INAUGURATION
56

FUN FACT
Impeached and tried by the Senate,
acquitted by a single vote.

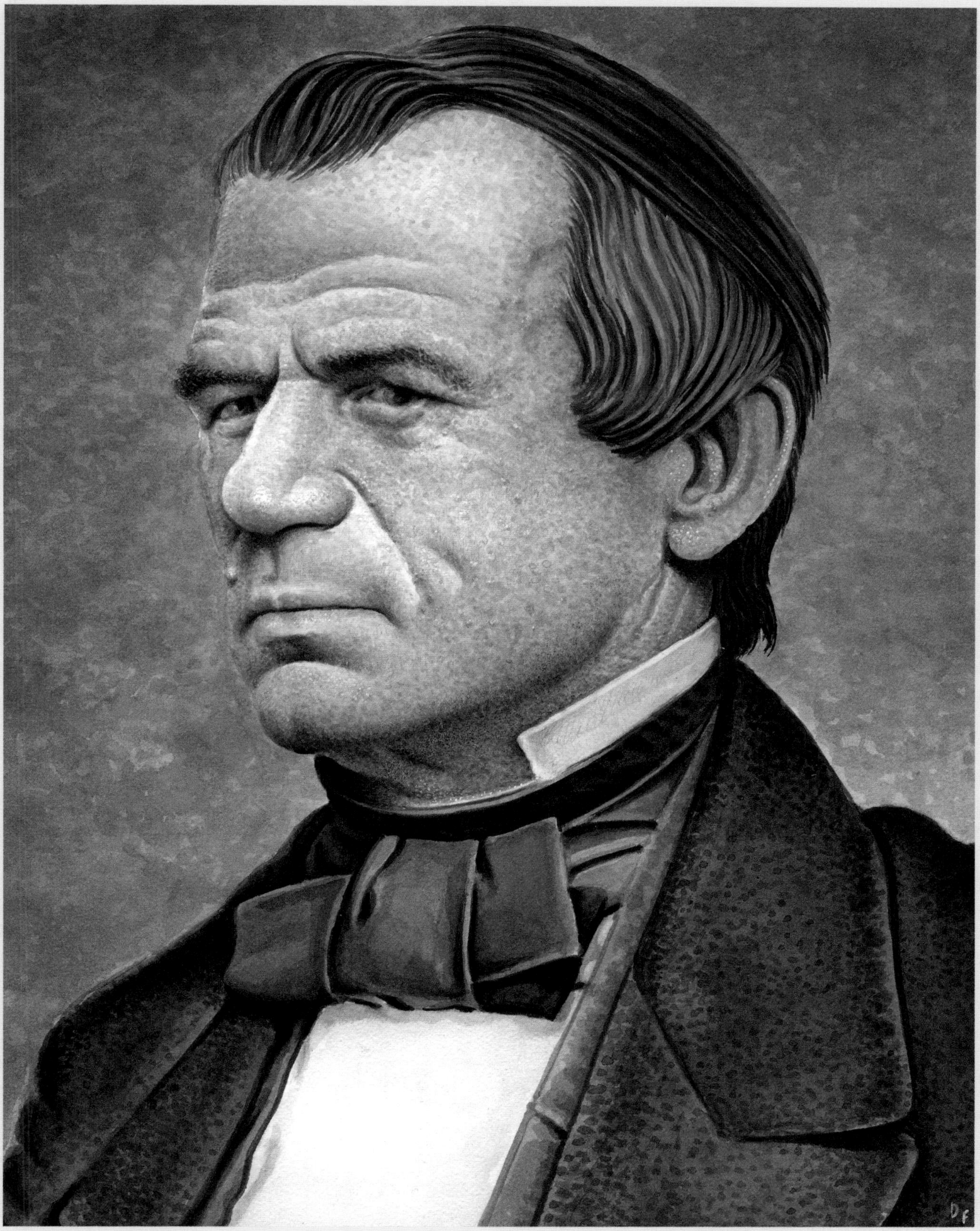

ULYSSES S. GRANT

BORN
April 27, 1822
Point Pleasant, Ohio

DIED
July 23, 1885

PARTY
Republican

TERM
1869–1877

AGE AT INAUGURATION
46

FUN FACT
Grant is not actually buried in Grant's tomb.
He is interred above ground in the largest
mausoleum in the United States.

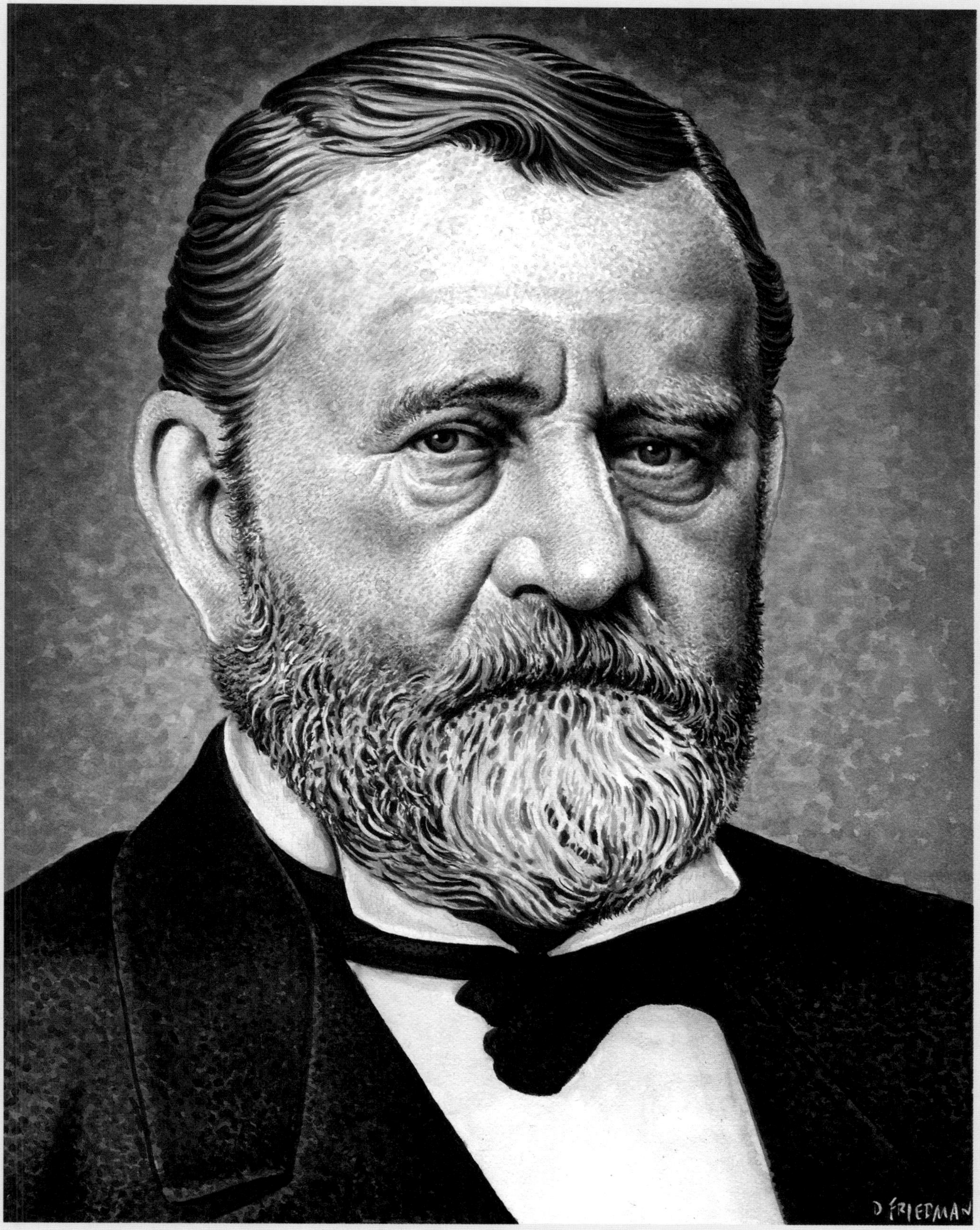
D FRIEDMAN

RUTHERFORD B. HAYES

BORN
October 4, 1822
Delaware, Ohio

DIED
January 17, 1893

PARTY
Republican

TERM
1877–1881

AGE AT INAUGURATION
54

FUN FACT
Hayes's wife, Lucy, was the first
First Lady to graduate from college.

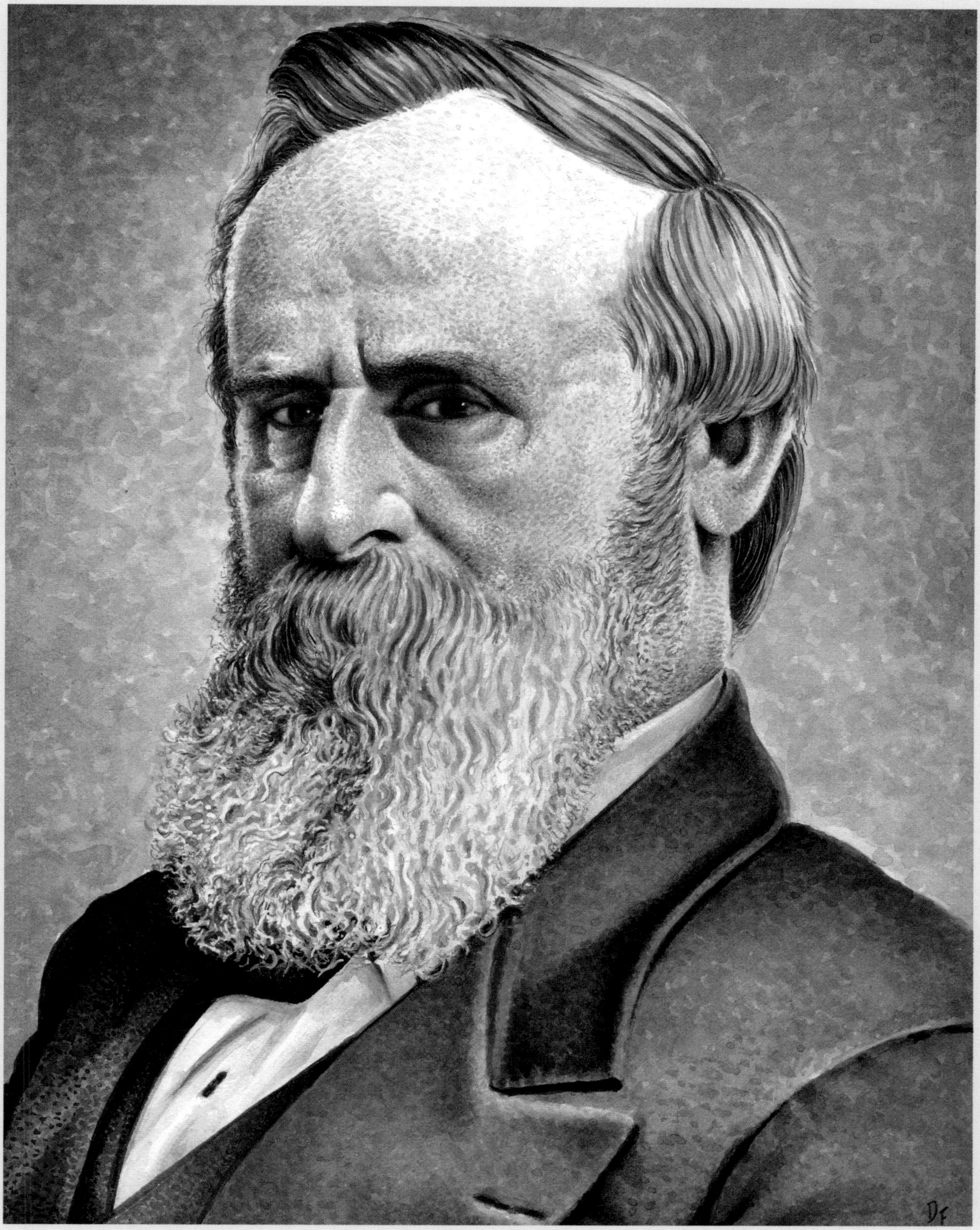
DF

20

JAMES A. GARFIELD

BORN
November 19, 1831
Orange, Ohio

DIED
September 19, 1881

PARTY
Republican

TERM
1881

AGE AT INAUGURATION
49

FUN FACT
The first left-handed president.

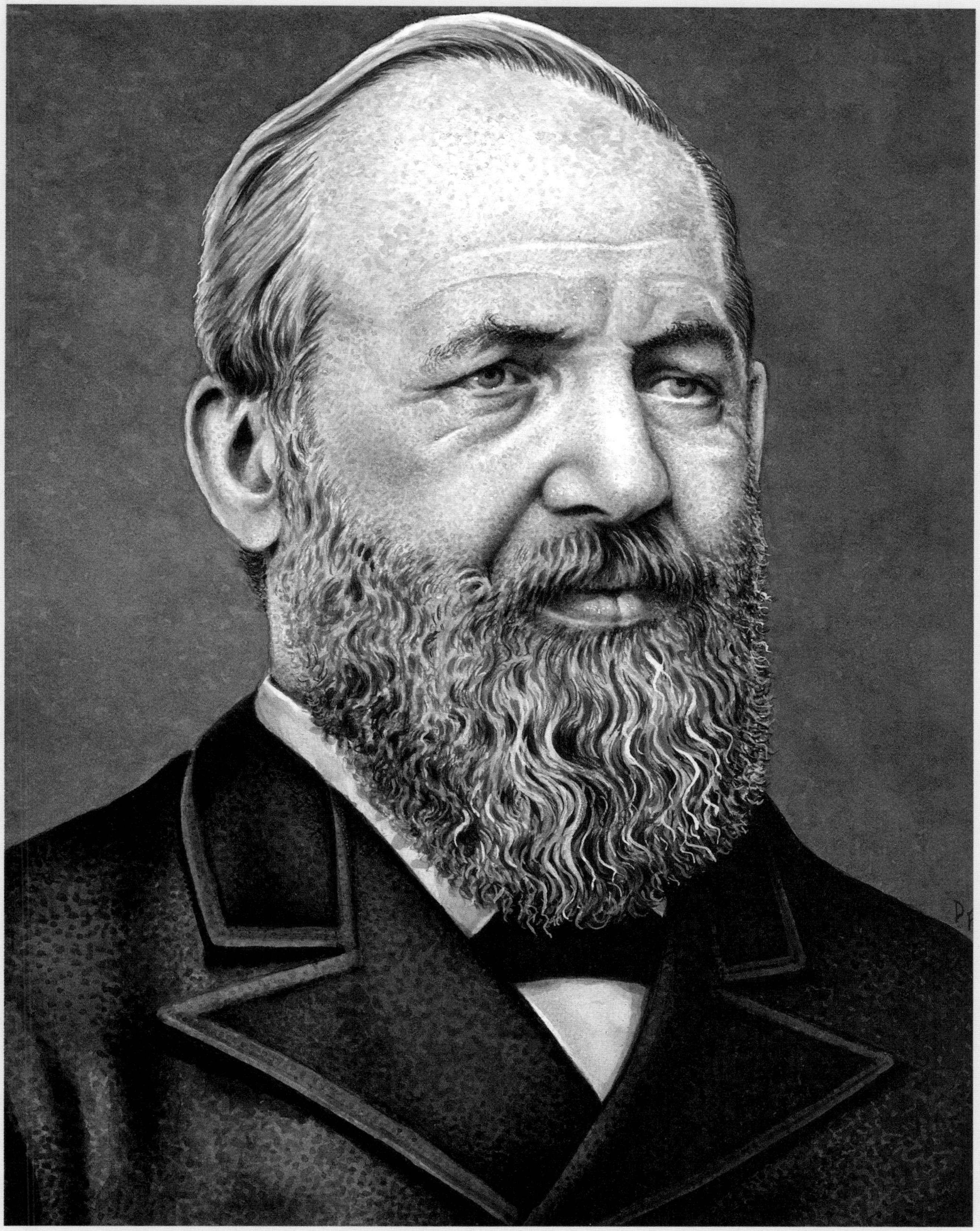

CHESTER A. ARTHUR

BORN
October 5, 1829
Fairfield, Vermont

DIED
November 18, 1886

PARTY
Republican

TERM
1881–1885

AGE AT INAUGURATION
51

FUN FACT
Arthur owned 80 pairs of pants and
changed his attire several times a day.

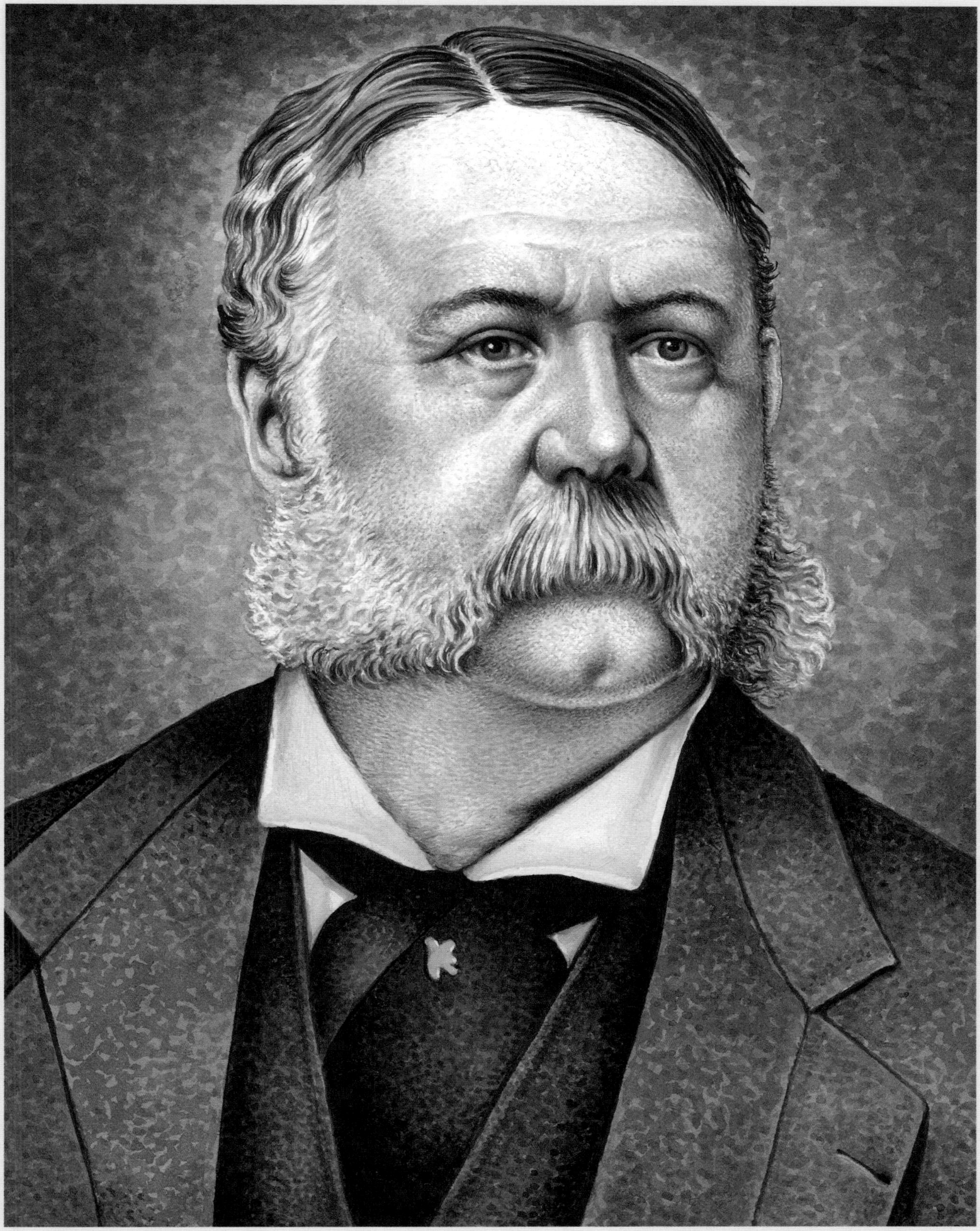

22 & 24

GROVER CLEVELAND

BORN
March 18, 1837
Caldwell, New Jersey

DIED
June 24, 1908

PARTY
Democratic

TERMS
1885–1889; 1893–1897

AGES WHEN INAUGURATED
47; 55

FUN FACT
Cleveland is the only president to be elected
to two non-consecutive terms.

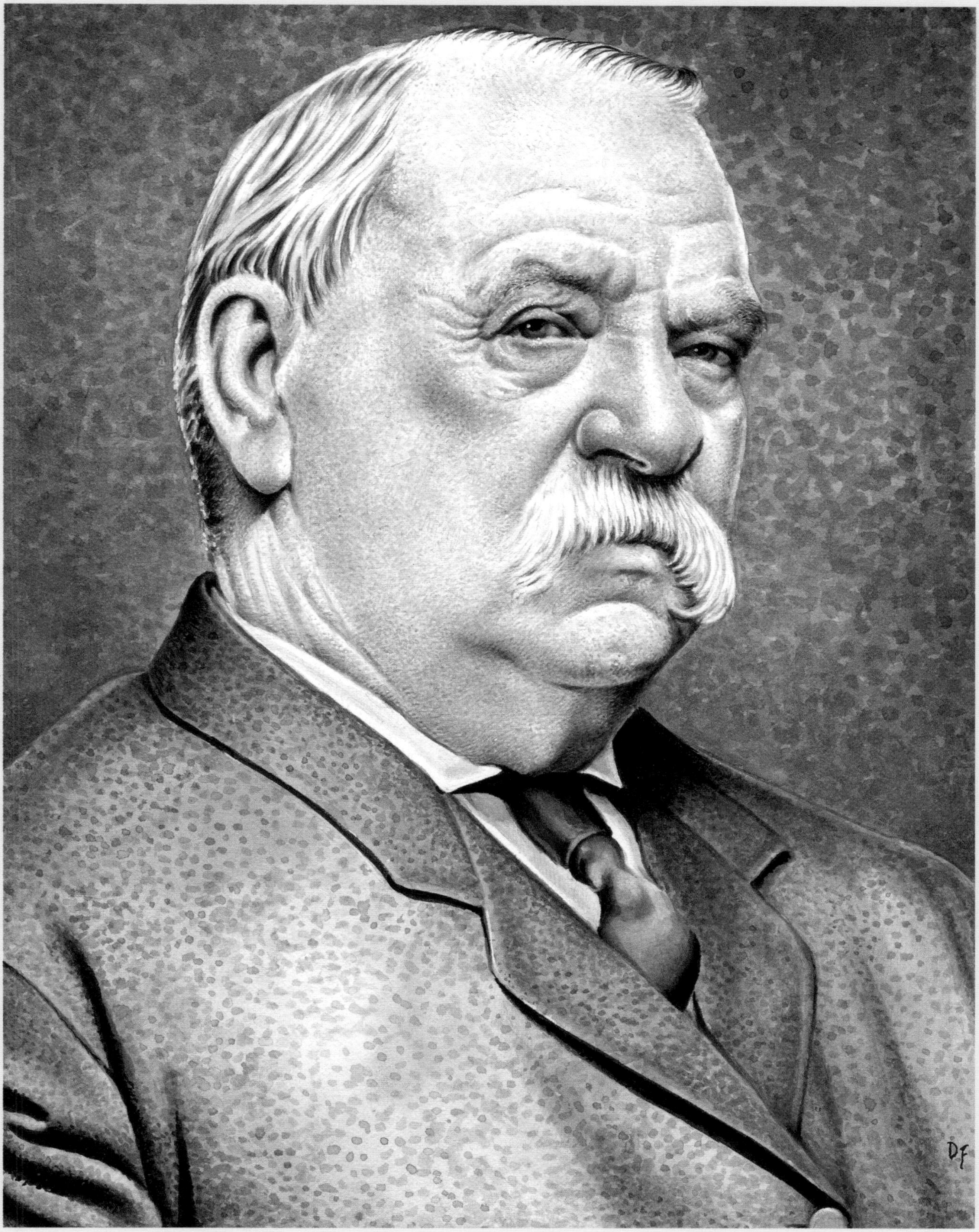
DF

23

BENJAMIN HARRISON

BORN
August 20, 1833
North Bend, Ohio

DIED
March 13, 1901

PARTY
Republican

TERM
1889–1893

AGE AT INAUGURATION
55

FUN FACT
The grandson of President William Henry Harrison.

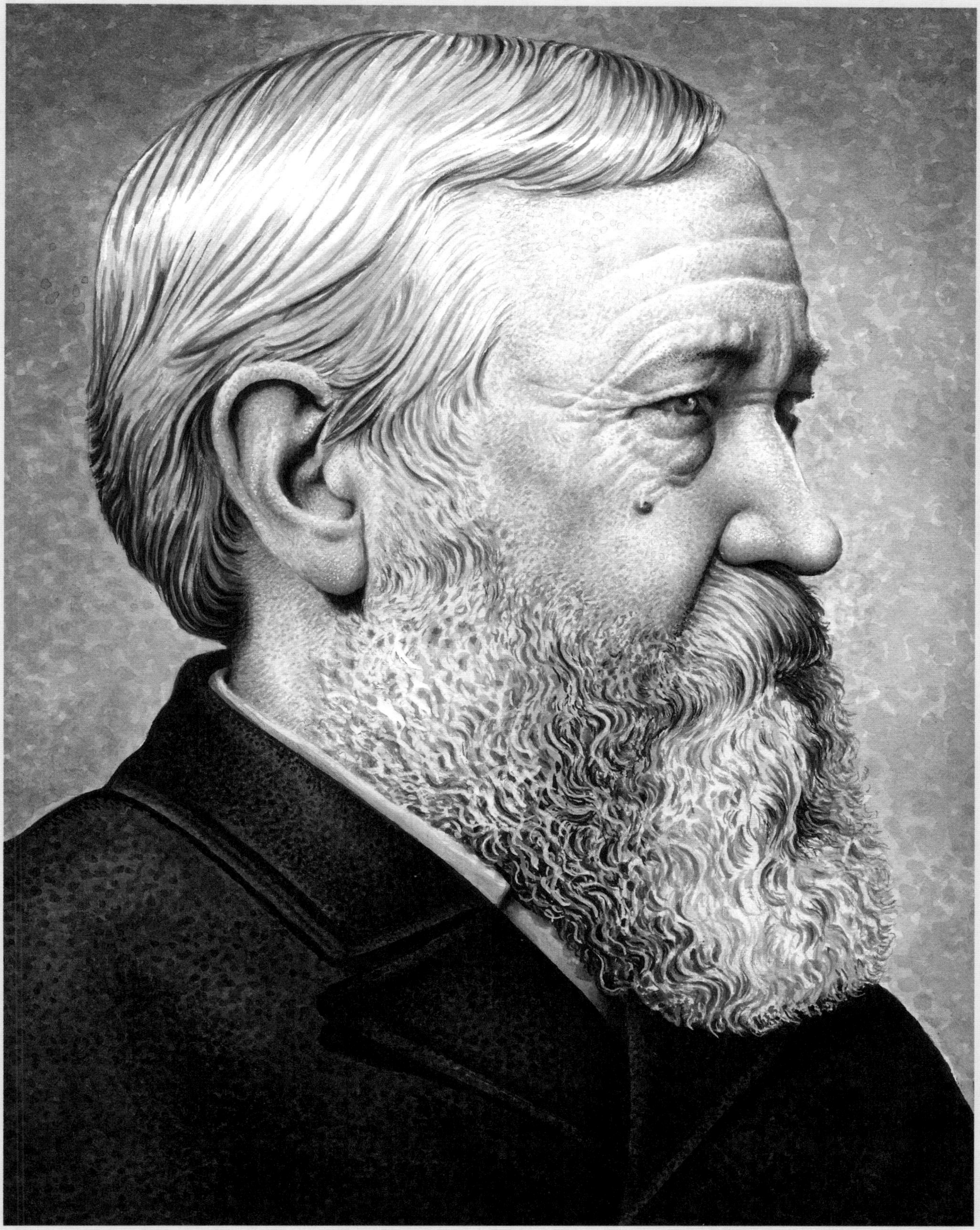

WILLIAM McKINLEY

BORN
January 29, 1843
Niles, Ohio

DIED
September 14, 1901

PARTY
Republican

TERM
1897–1901

AGE AT INAUGURATION
54

FUN FACT
McKinley's portrait was on the $500 bill
from 1945 to 1969.

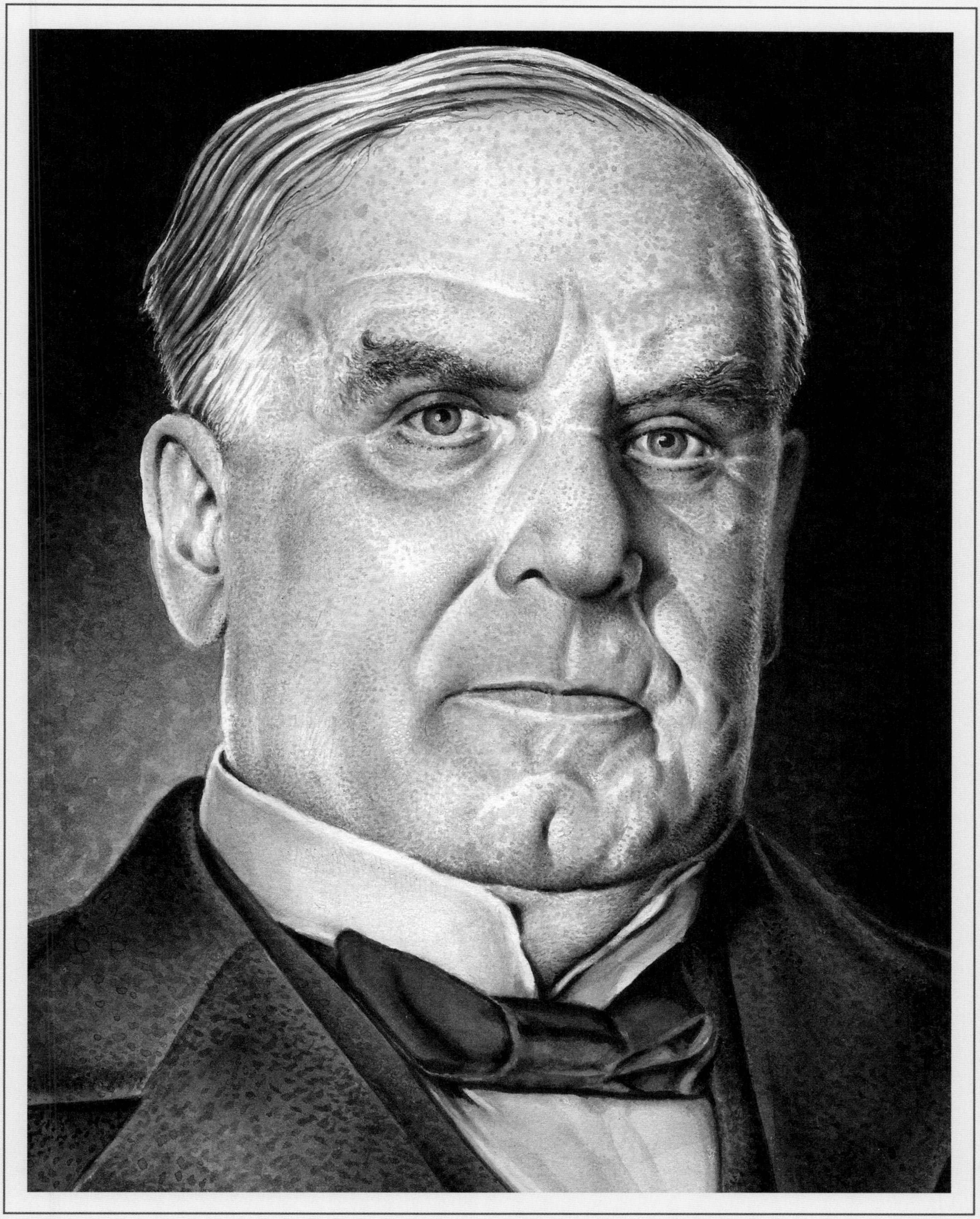

THEODORE ROOSEVELT

BORN
October 27, 1858
New York, New York

DIED
January 6, 1919

PARTY
Republican

TERM
1901–1909

AGE AT INAUGURATION
42

FUN FACT
The first president to visit a foreign country while in office.

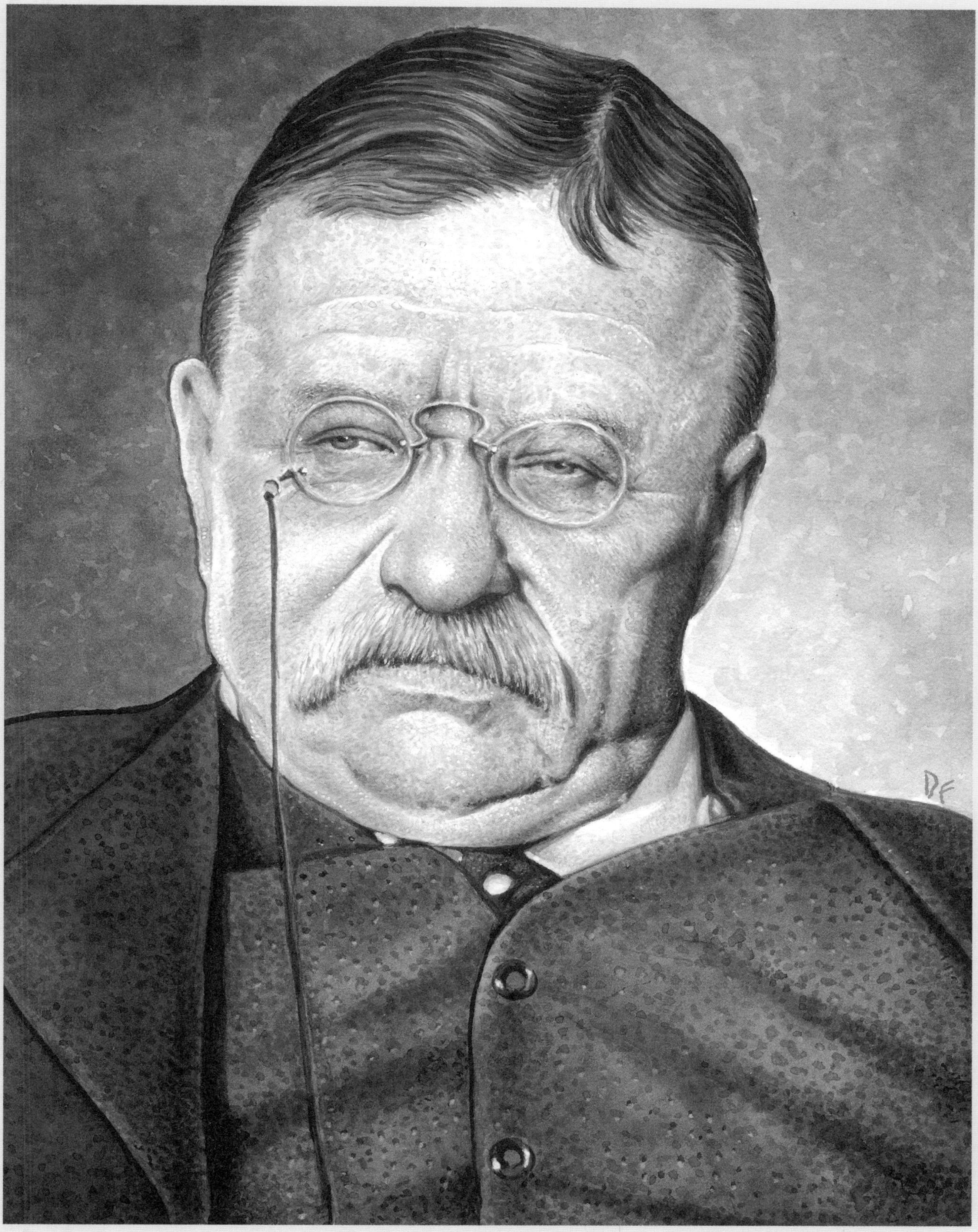

WILLIAM HOWARD TAFT

BORN
September 15, 1857
Cincinnati, Ohio

DIED
March 8, 1930

PARTY
Republican

TERM
1909–1913

AGE AT INAUGURATION
51

FUN FACT
At 354 pounds, Taft was the heaviest president.

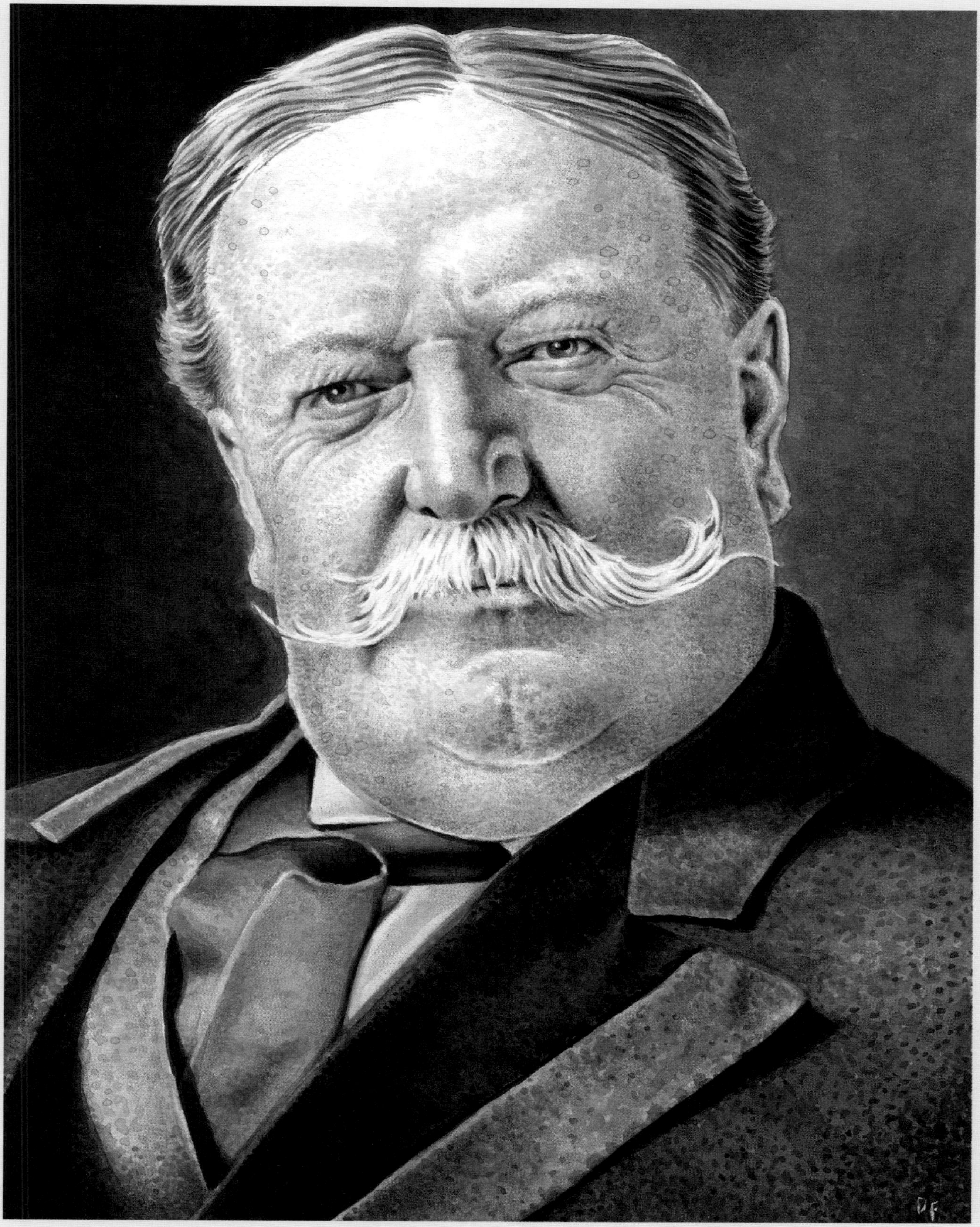
DF

WOODROW WILSON

BORN
December 28, 1856
Staunton, Virginia

DIED
February 3, 1924

PARTY
Democratic

TERM
1913–1921

AGE AT INAUGURATION
56

FUN FACT
The first president to hold a news conference.

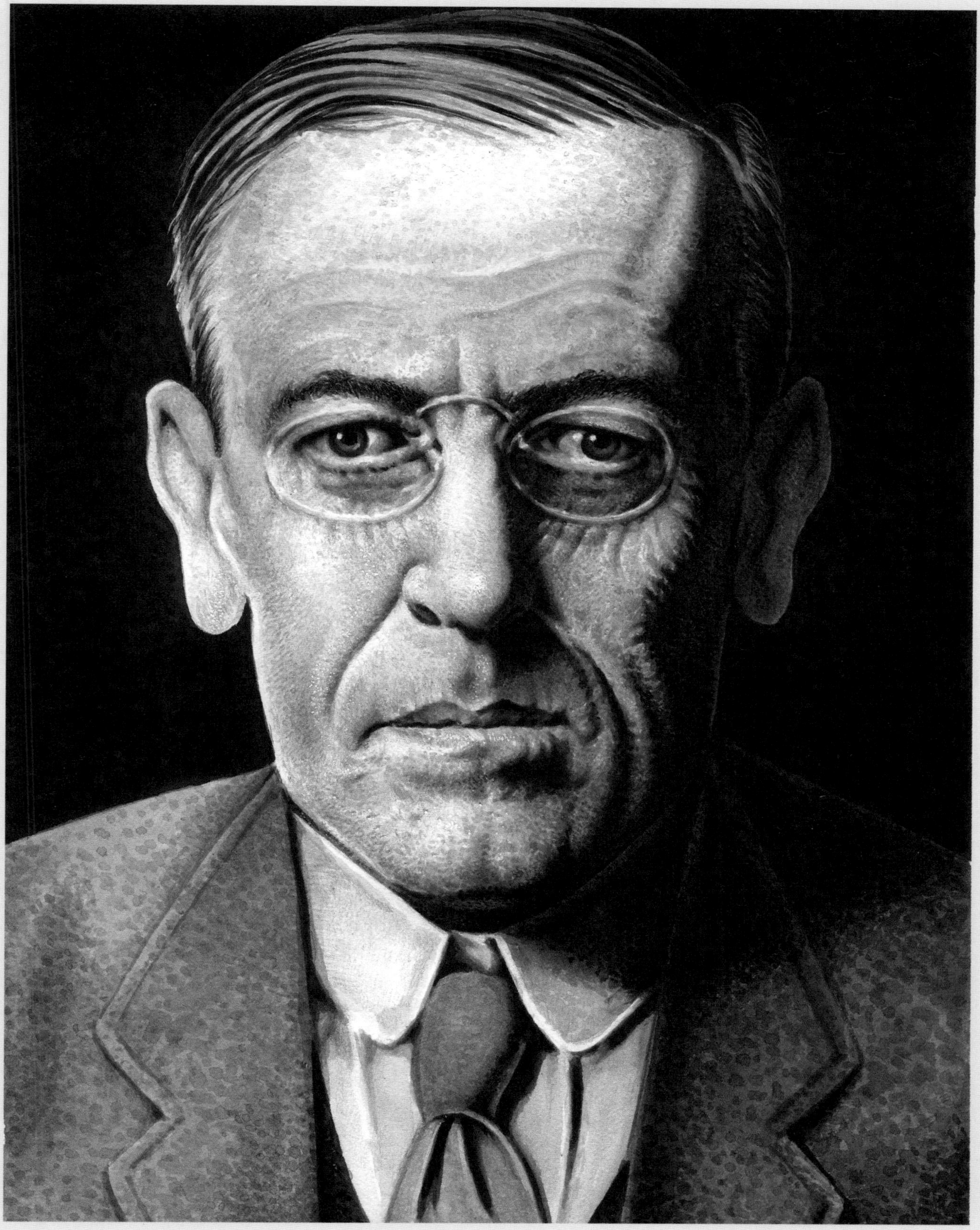

WARREN G. HARDING

BORN
November 2, 1865
near Blooming Grove, Ohio

DIED
August 2, 1923

PARTY
Republican

TERM
1921–1923

AGE AT INAUGURATION
55

FUN FACT
Elected in the first election in which women voted.

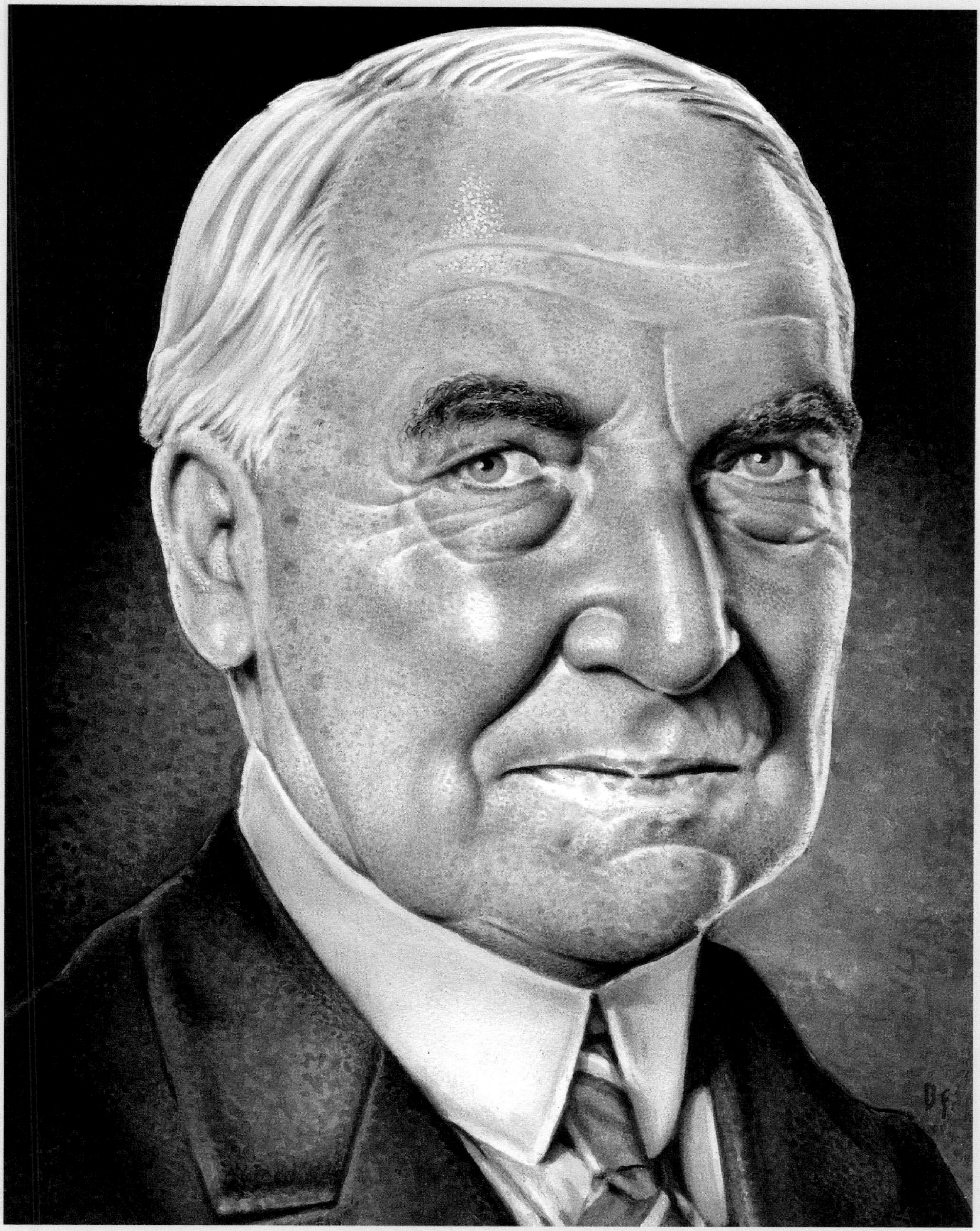

CALVIN COOLIDGE

BORN
July 4, 1872
Plymouth Notch, Vermont

DIED
January 5, 1933

PARTY
Republican

TERM
1923–1929

AGE AT INAUGURATION
51

FUN FACT
A journalist once reportedly challenged Coolidge,
"I bet my editor I could get more than two words out of you,"
to which Coolidge allegedly replied, "You lose."

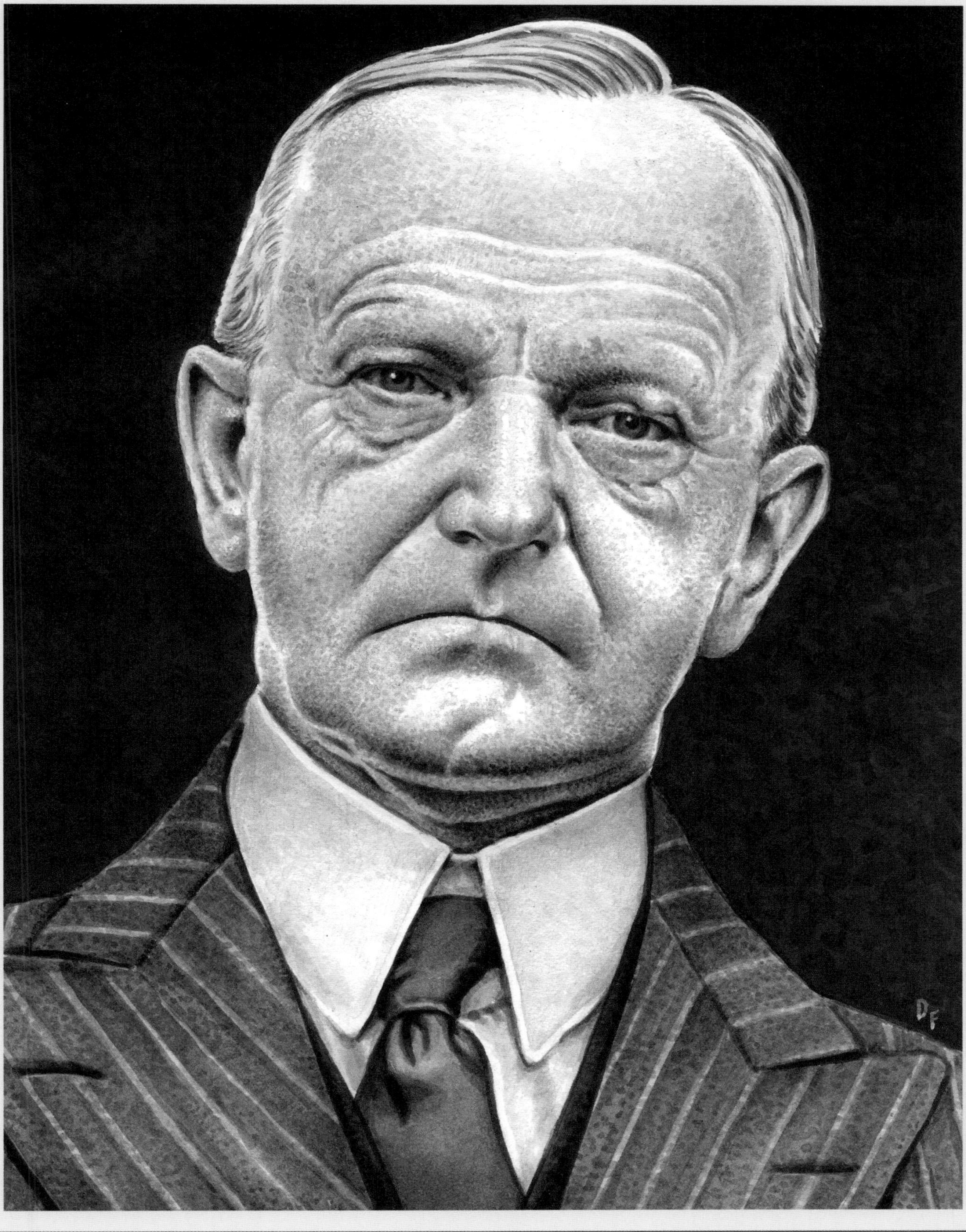

31

HERBERT C. HOOVER

BORN
August 10, 1874
West Branch, Iowa

DIED
October 20, 1964

PARTY
Republican

TERM
1929–1933

AGE AT INAUGURATION
54

FUN FACT
The first sitting U.S. president to stay at
New York's Waldorf Astoria hotel; he later
died in a suite in the hotel, in 1964.

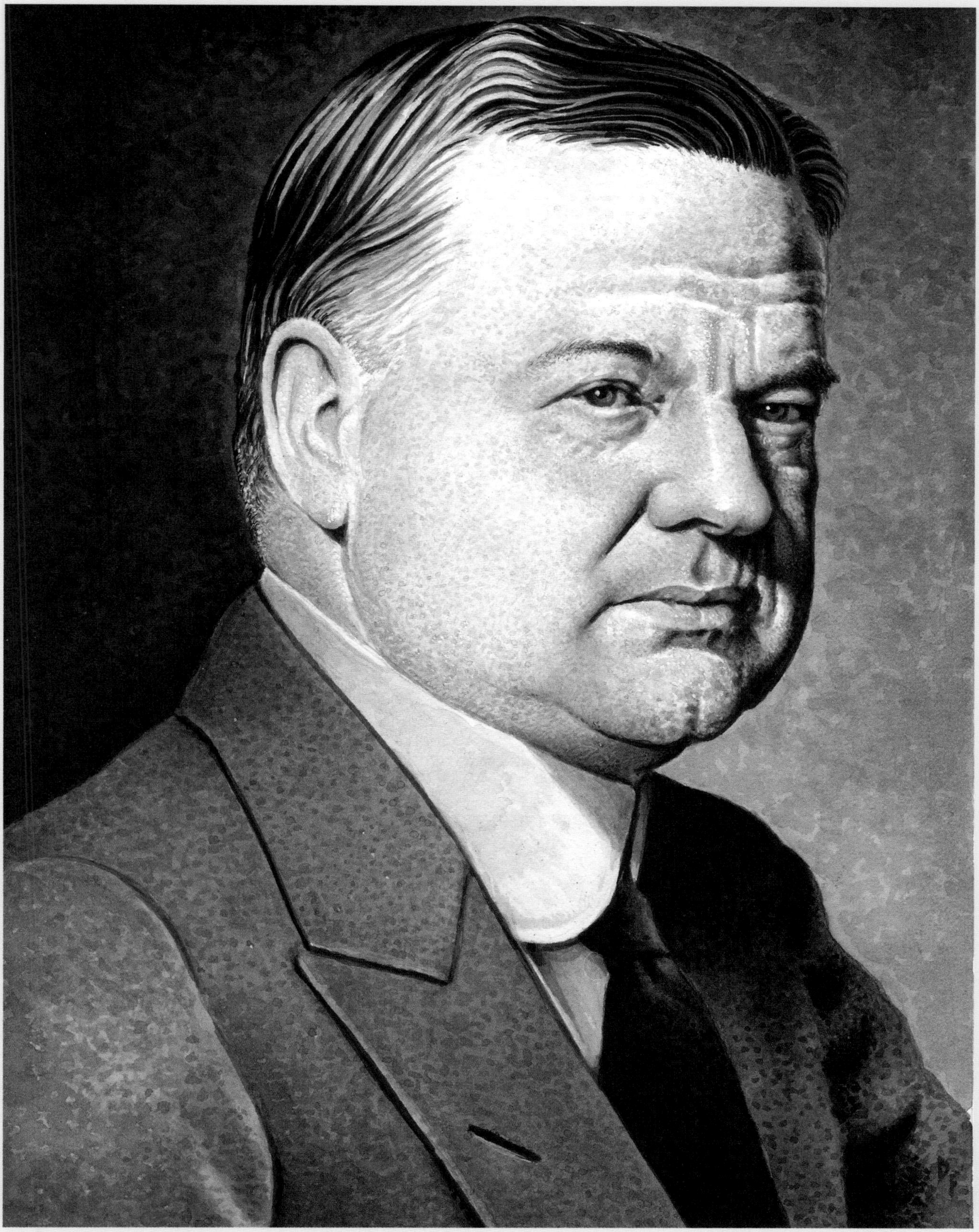

FRANKLIN D. ROOSEVELT

BORN
January 30, 1882
Hyde Park, New York

DIED
April 12, 1945

PARTY
Democratic

TERM
1933–1945

AGE AT INAUGURATION
51

FUN FACT
The only president elected four times.

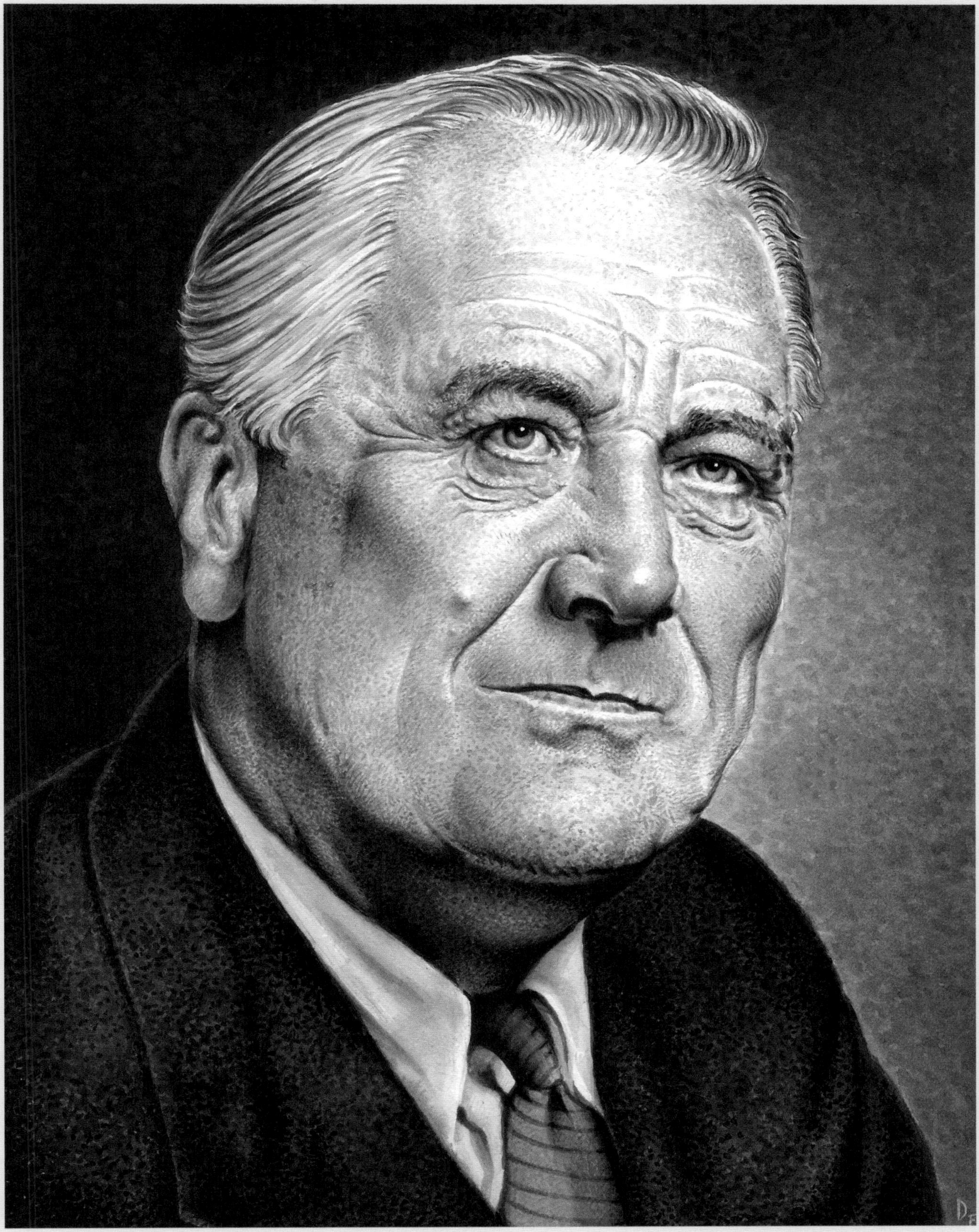

HARRY S. TRUMAN

BORN
May 8, 1884
Lamar, Missouri

DIED
December 26, 1972

PARTY
Democratic

TERM
1945–1953

AGE AT INAUGURATION
60

FUN FACT
The "S" does not stand for anything.

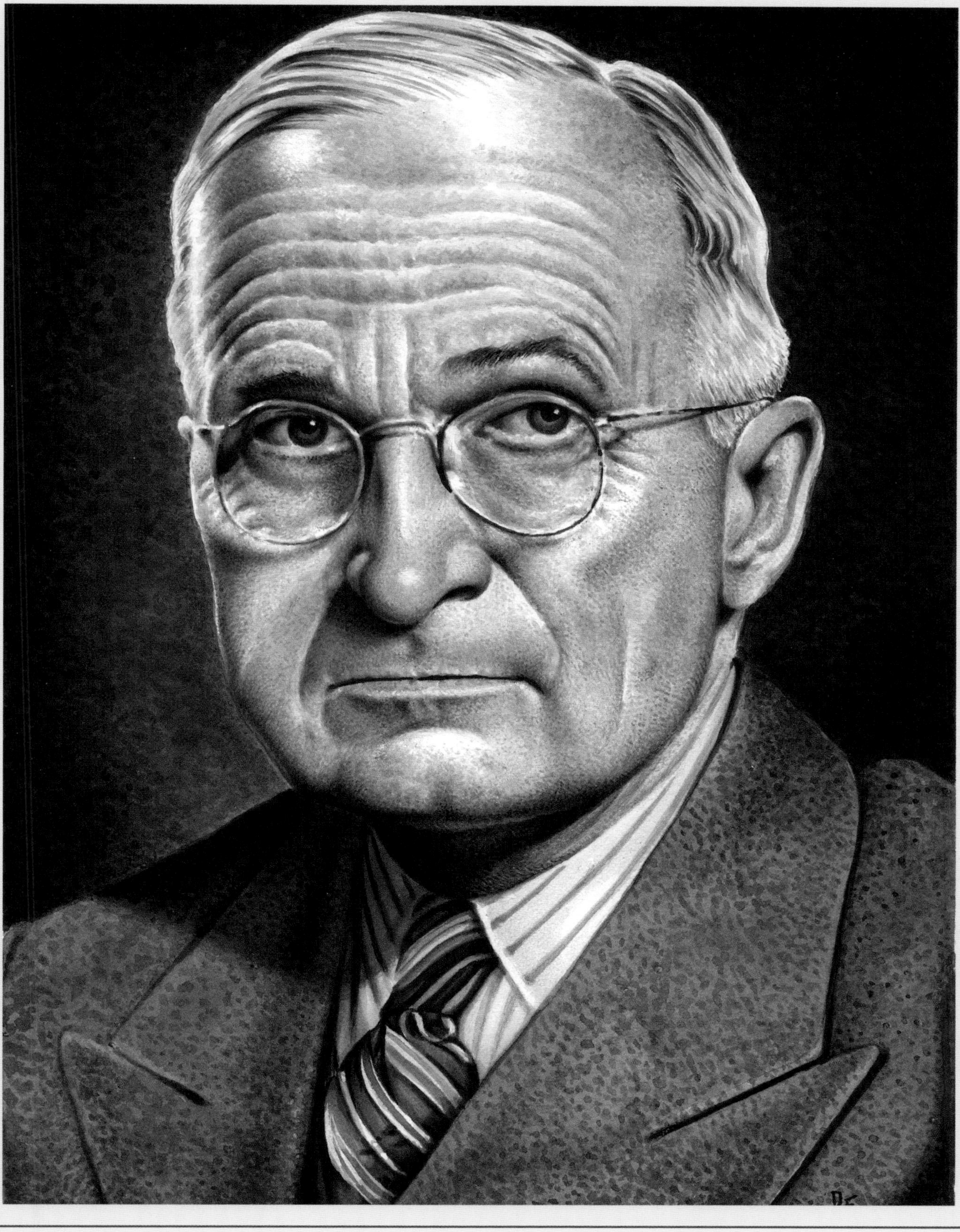

DWIGHT D. EISENHOWER

BORN
October 14, 1890
Denison, Texas

DIED
March 28, 1969

PARTY
Republican

TERM
1953–1961

AGE AT INAUGURATION
62

FUN FACT
Named the presidential retreat
Camp David after his grandson.

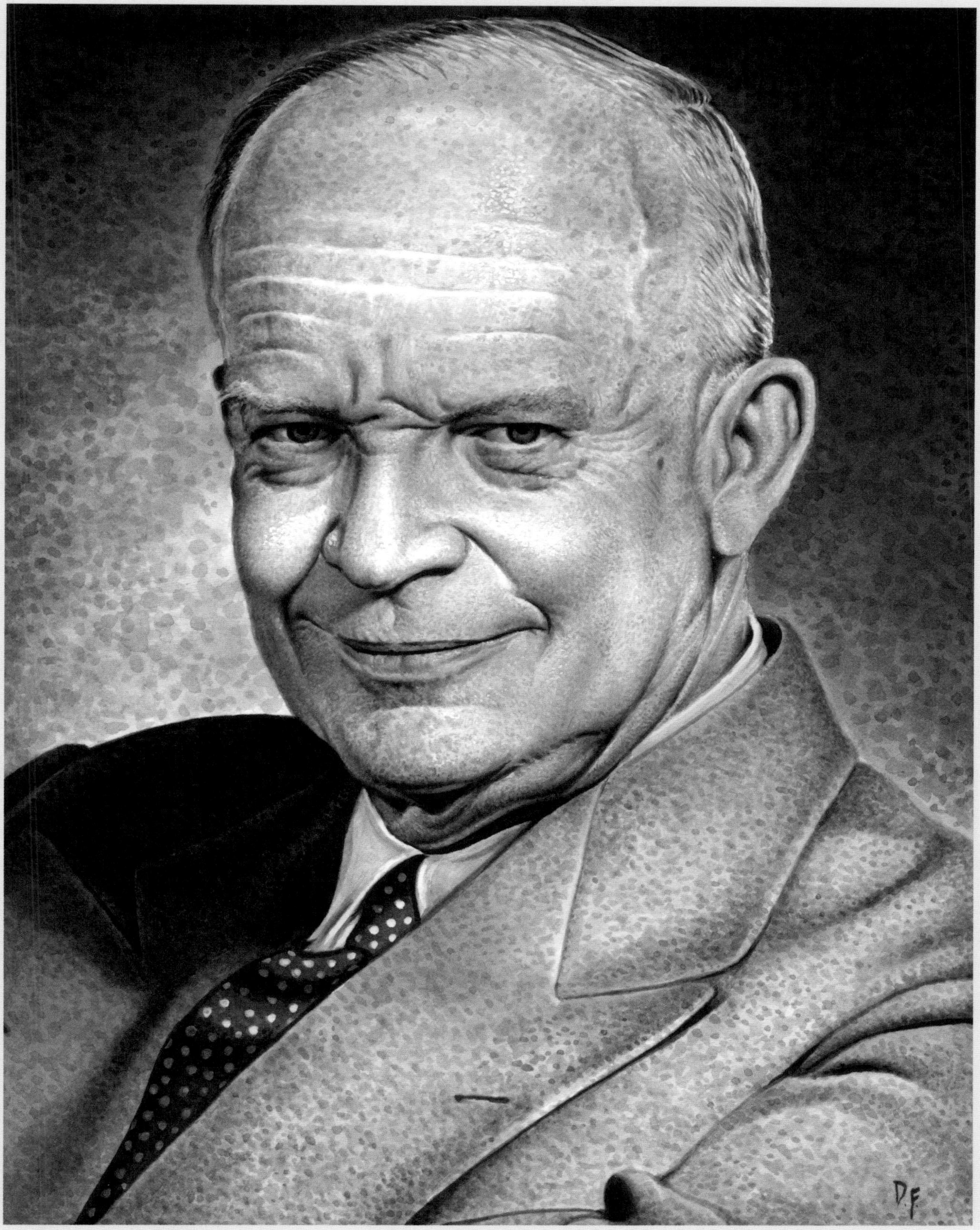
D.F

JOHN F. KENNEDY

BORN
May 29, 1917
Brookline, Massachusetts

DIED
November 22, 1963

PARTY
Democratic

TERM
1961–1963

AGE AT INAUGURATION
43

FUN FACT
The first president who had been a boy scout.

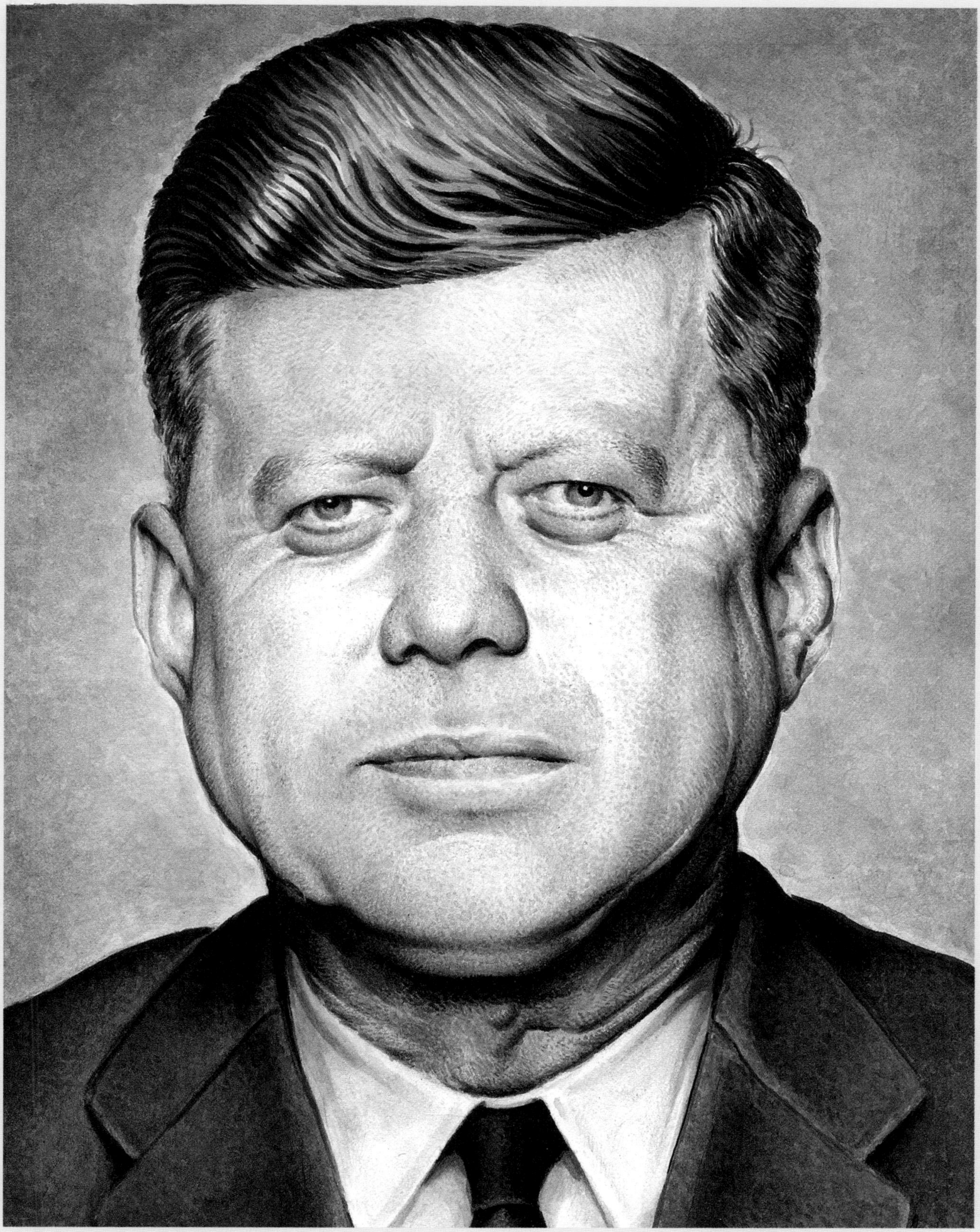

LYNDON B. JOHNSON

BORN
August 27, 1908
Stonewall, Texas

DIED
January 22, 1973

PARTY
Democratic

TERM
1963–1969

AGE AT INAUGURATION
55

FUN FACT
Johnson's two Beagles, "Him" and "Her," lived in the
White House while he served as president.

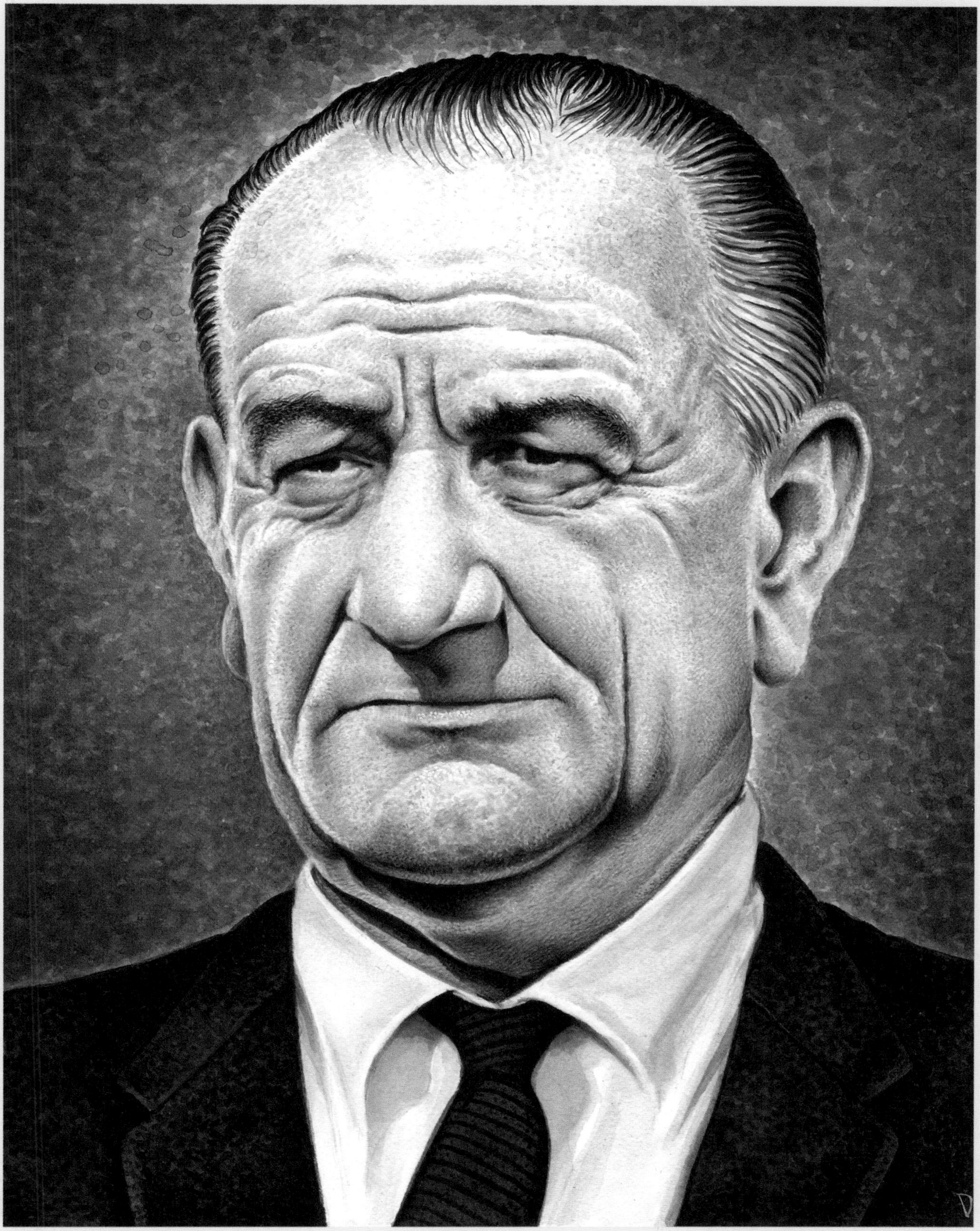

RICHARD M. NIXON

BORN
January 9, 1913
Yorba Linda, California

DIED
April 22, 1994

PARTY
Republican

TERM
1969–1974

AGE AT INAUGURATION
56

FUN FACT
Nixon could play five musical instruments:
piano, saxophone, clarinet, accordion, and violin.

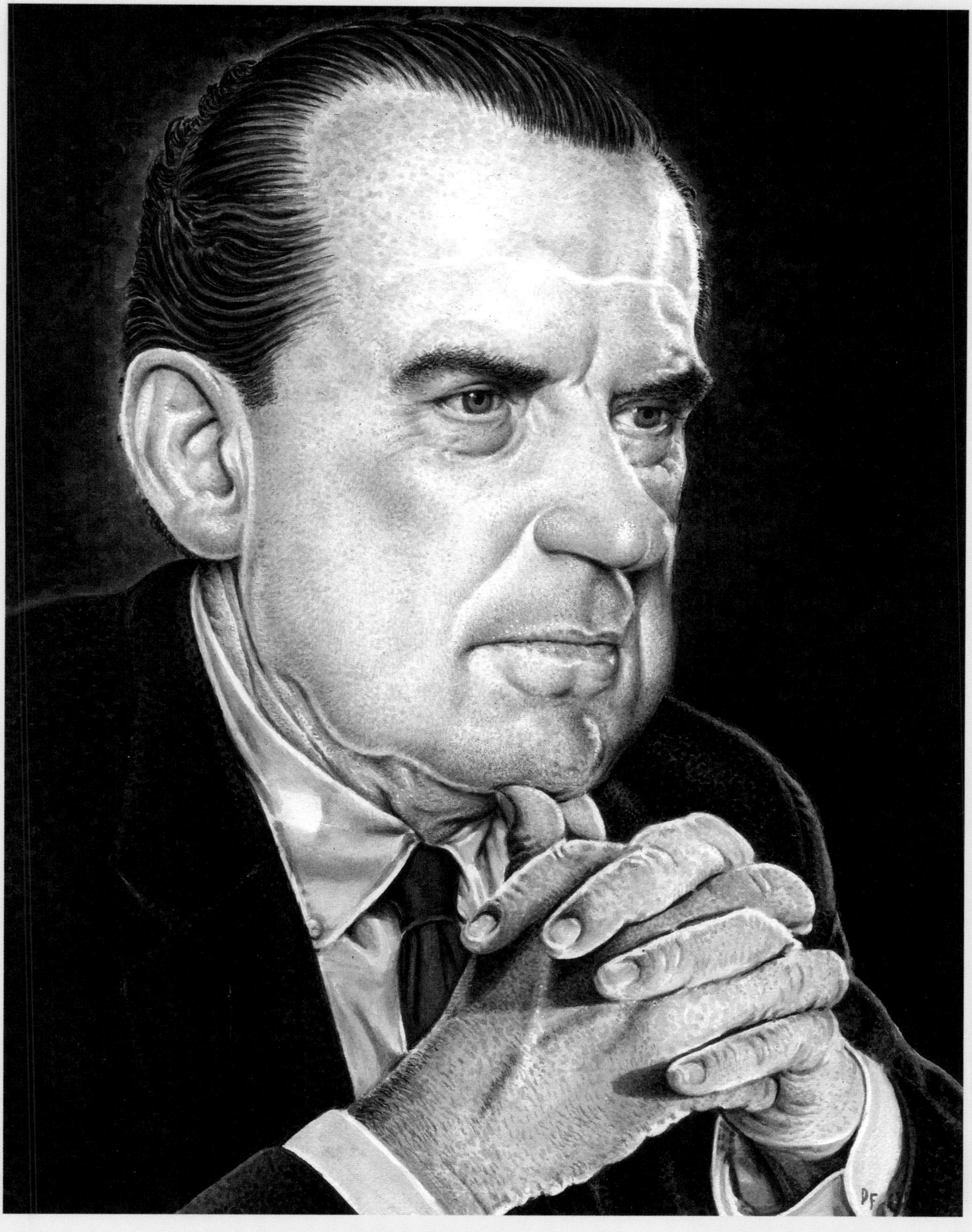

GERALD R. FORD

BORN
July 14, 1913
Omaha, Nebraska

DIED
December 26, 2006

PARTY
Republican

TERM
1974–1977

AGE AT INAUGURATION
61

FUN FACT
George Harrison became the first ex-Beatle to enter
the White House, visiting president Ford in 1974.

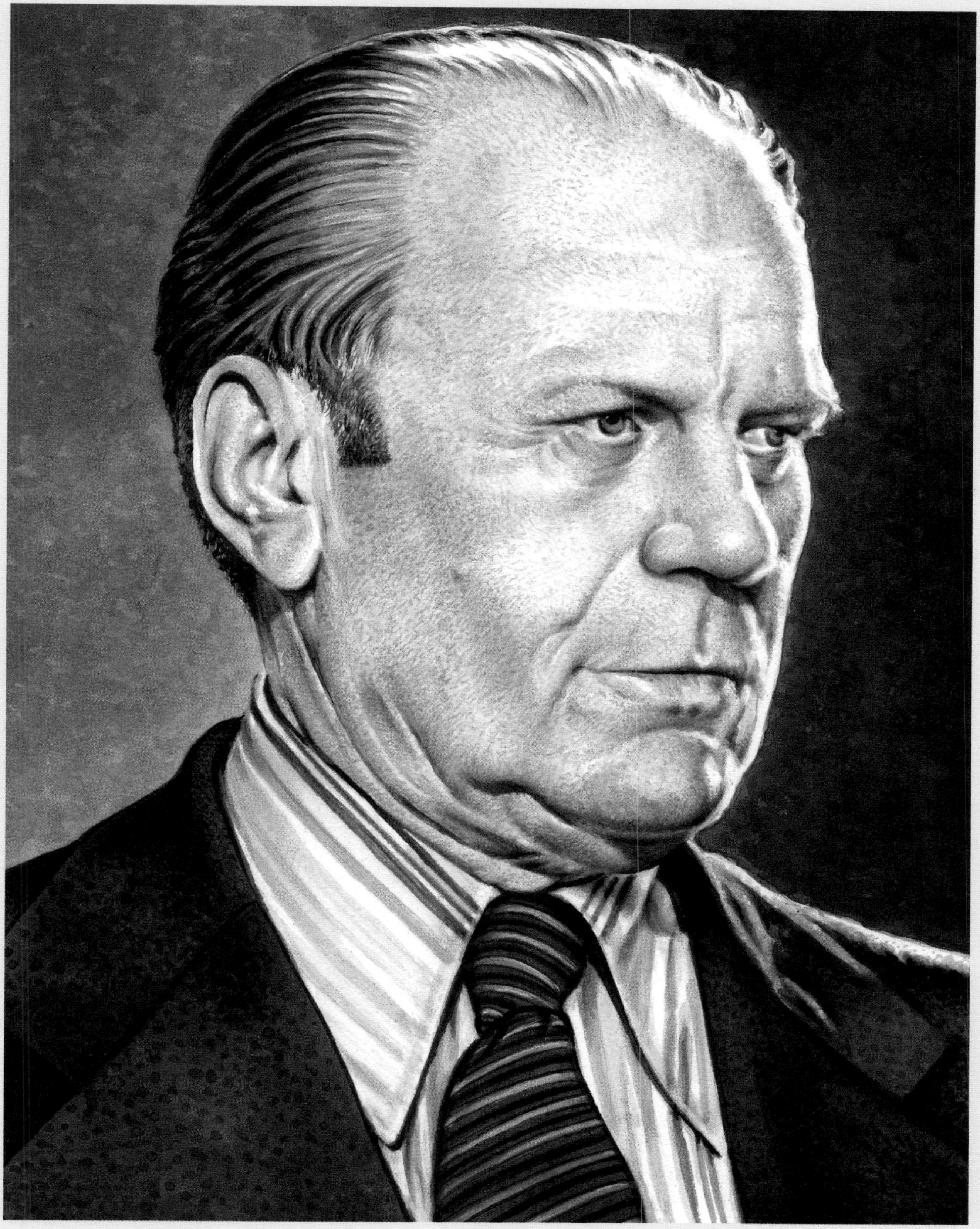

JAMES (JIMMY) E. CARTER

BORN
October 1, 1924
Plains, Georgia

PARTY
Democratic

TERM
1977–1981

AGE AT INAUGURATION
52

FUN FACT
The first president born in a hospital.

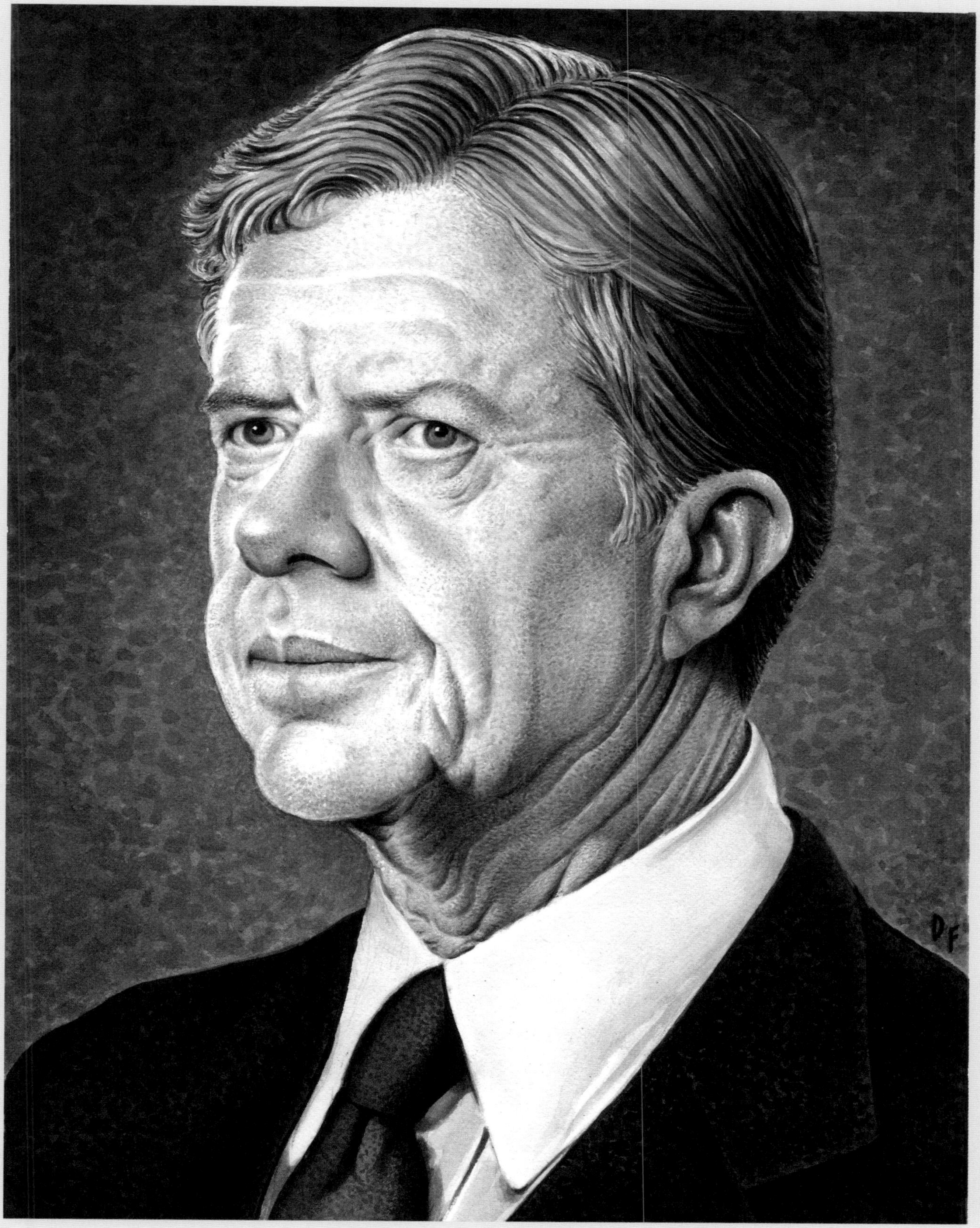
DF

RONALD W. REAGAN

BORN
February 6, 1911
Tampico, Illinois

DIED
June 5, 2004

PARTY
Republican

TERM
1981–1989

AGE AT INAUGURATION
69

FUN FACT
The first president who once co-starred
with a chimp in a motion picture.

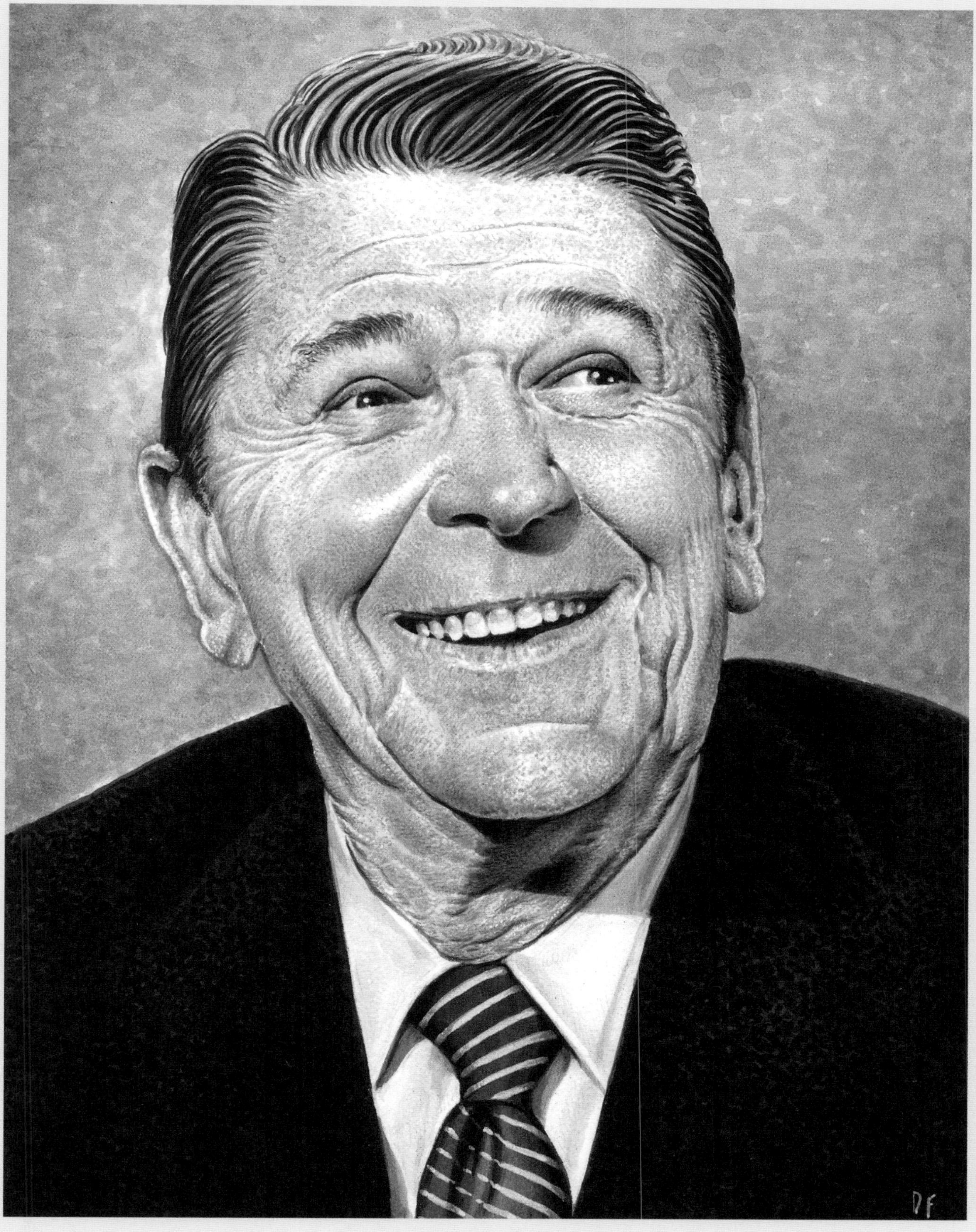
DF

GEORGE H. W. BUSH

BORN
June 12, 1924
Milton, Massachusetts

PARTY
Republican

TERM
1989–1993

AGE AT INAUGURATION
64

FUN FACT
Bush was the first sitting vice president
to become President since Martin Van Buren.

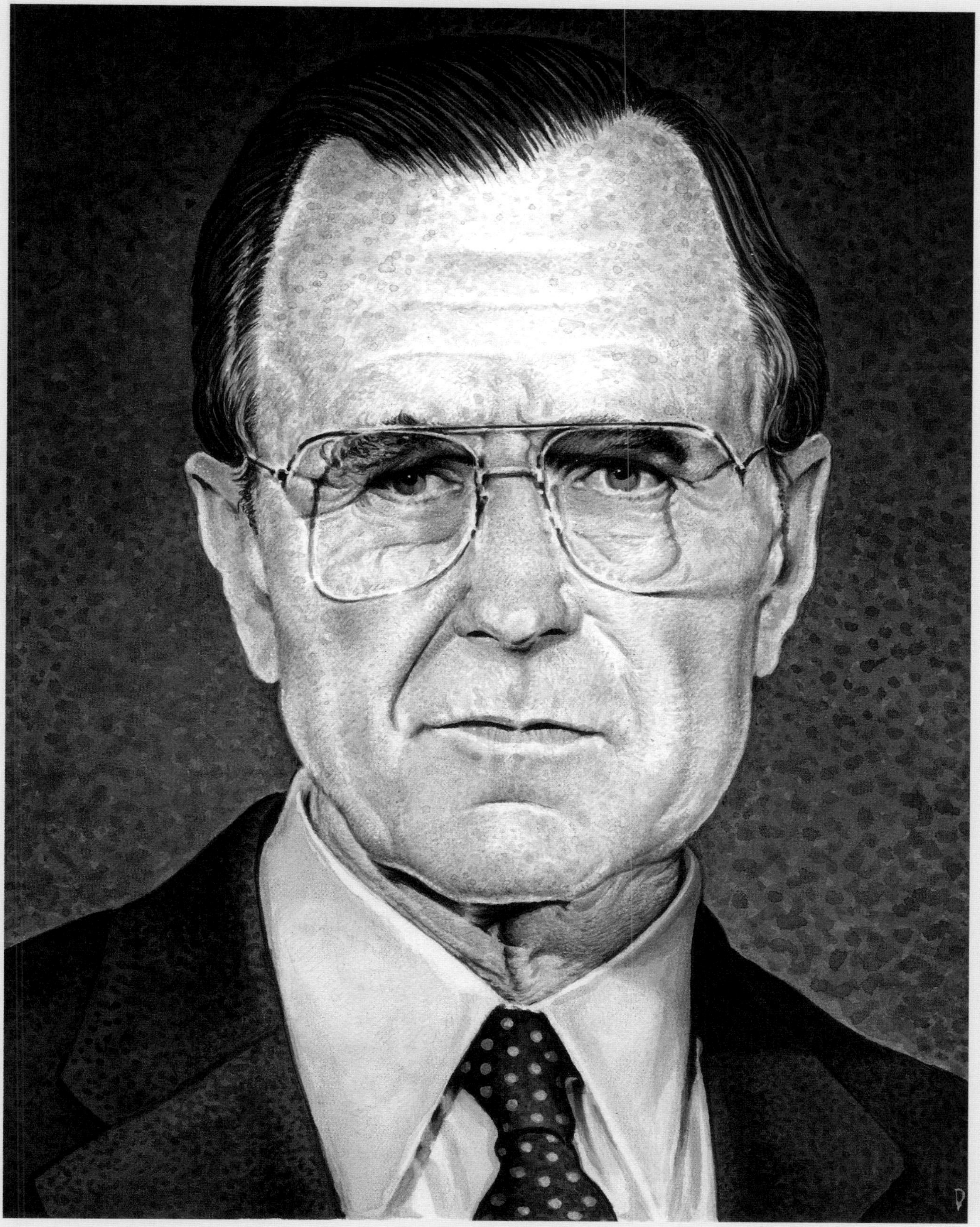

WILLIAM (BILL) J. CLINTON

BORN
August 19, 1946
Hope, Arkansas

PARTY
Democratic

TERM
1993–2001

AGE AT INAUGURATION
46

FUN FACT
The first president to win a Grammy award
for Best Spoken Word Album.

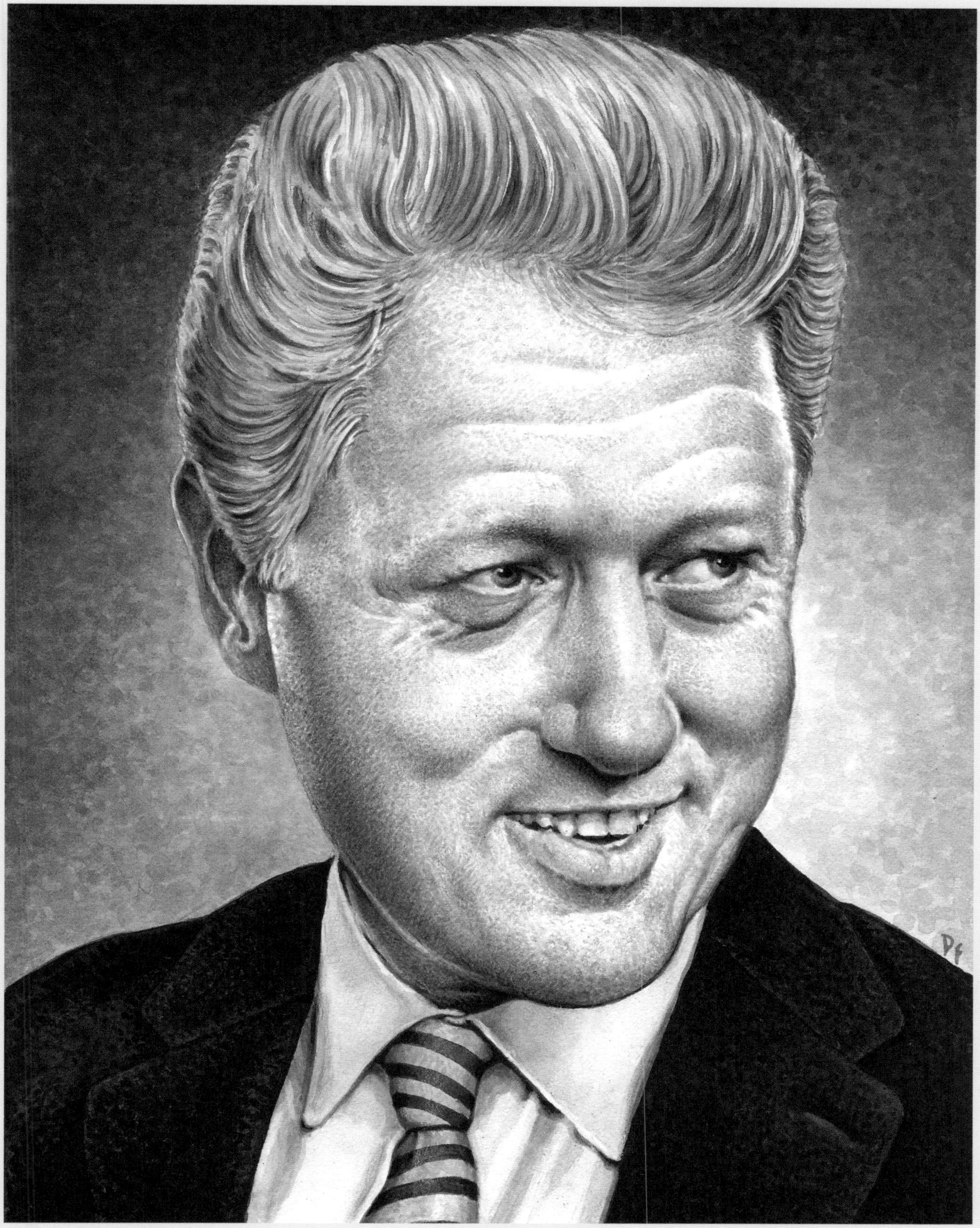

GEORGE W. BUSH

BORN
July 6, 1946
New Haven, Connecticut

PARTY
Republican

TERM
2001–2009

AGE AT INAUGURATION
54

FUN FACT
The first president to finish a marathon.

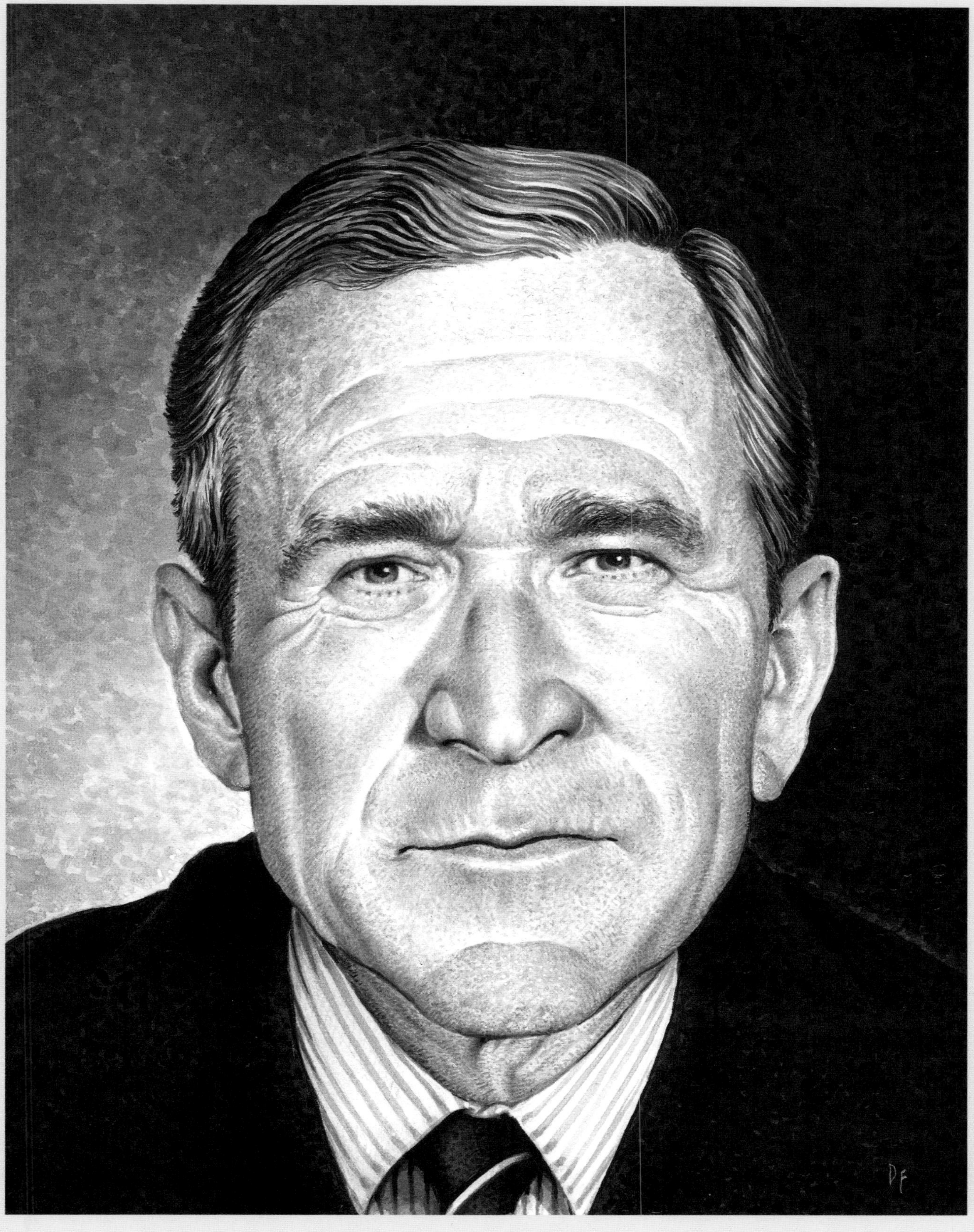
DF

BARACK OBAMA

BORN
August 4, 1961
Honolulu, Hawaii

PARTY
Democrat

TERM
2009–2017

AGE AT INAUGURATION
47

FUN FACT
Was a self-described comic book
collector growing up.

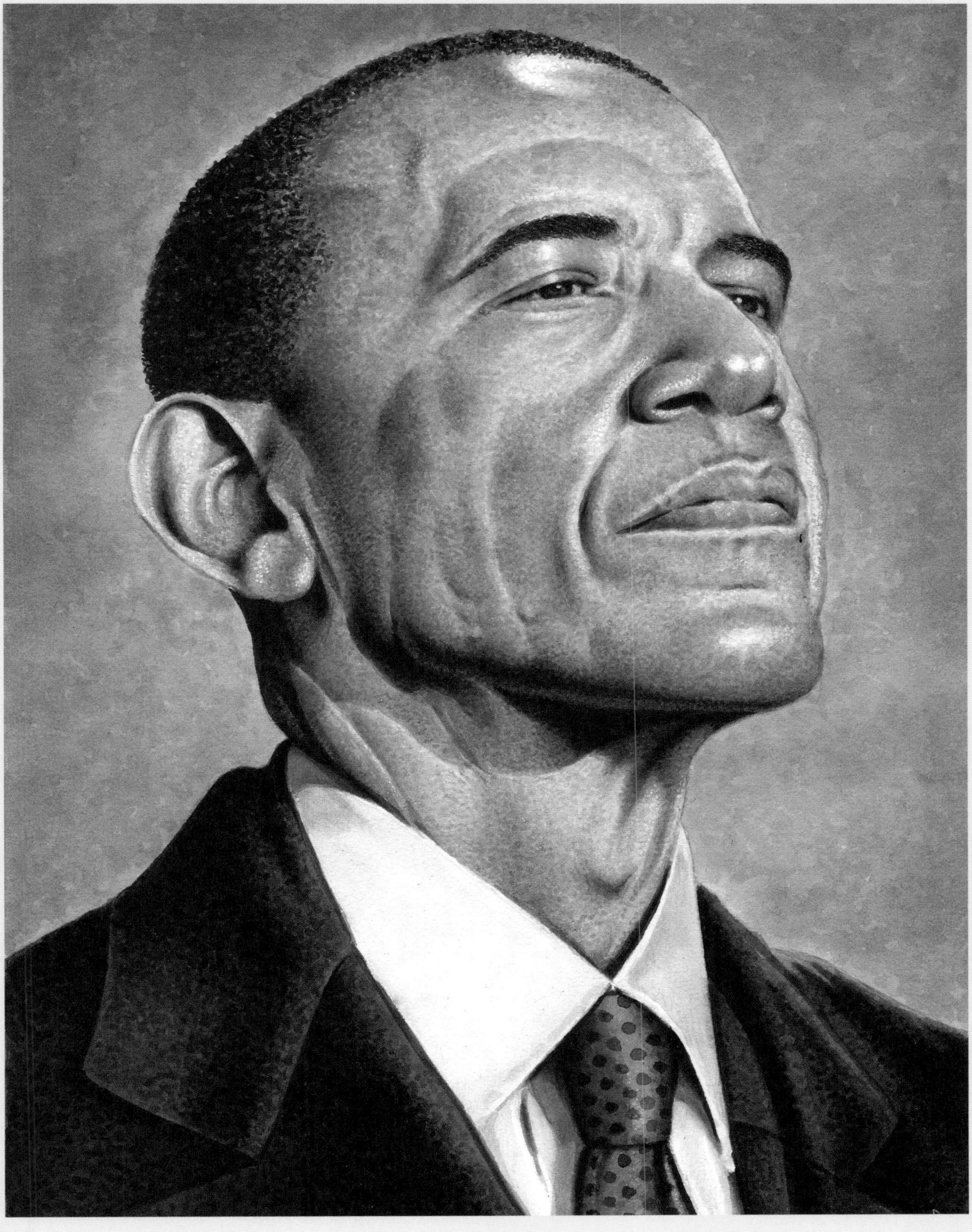

DONALD J. TRUMP

BORN
June 14, 1946
New York City, NY

PARTY
Republican

TERM
2017-present

AGE AT INAUGURATION
70

FUN FACT
The first president to host a reality
TV series that featured Gilbert Gottfried.

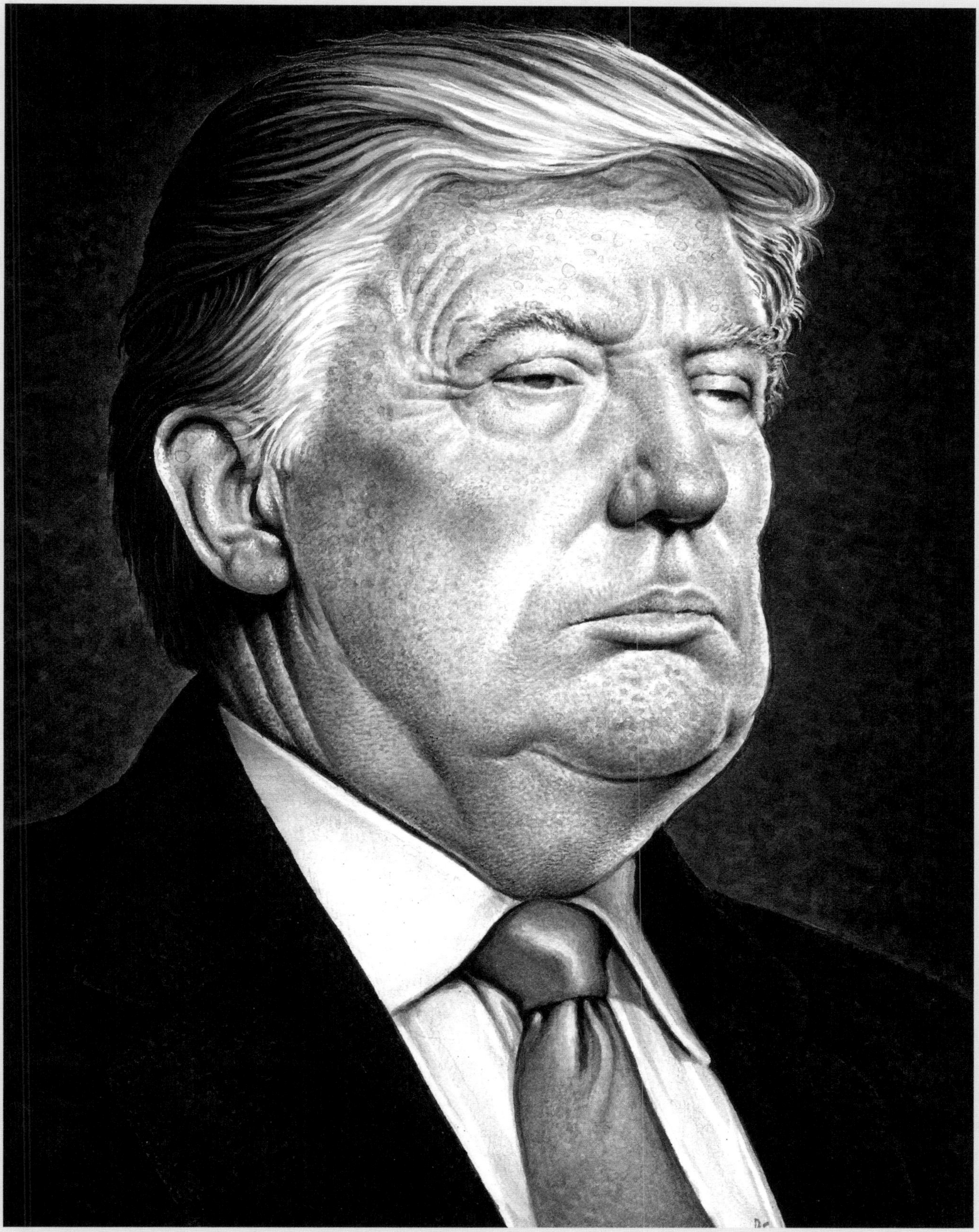

ALSO BY DREW FRIEDMAN

Any Similarity to Persons Living or Dead is Purely Coincidental,
(cowritten by Josh Alan Friedman). Fantagraphics Books, 1986 & 2012

Warts and All, (cowritten by Josh Alan Friedman).
Penguin, 1990, Fantagraphics Books, 1994

Private Lives of Public Figures, St. Martin's Press, 1993

Old Jewish Comedians, Fantagraphics Books, 2006

The Fun Never Stops!, Fantagraphics Books, 2007

More Old Jewish Comedians, Fantagraphics Books, 2008

Too Soon?, Fantagraphics Books, 2010

Even More Old Jewish Comedians, Fantagraphics Books, 2011

Drew Friedman's Sideshow Freaks, Blast Books, 2011

Heroes of the Comics, Fantagraphics Books, 2014

More Heroes of the Comics, Fantagraphics Books, 2016

Drew Friedman's Chosen People, Fantagraphics Books, 2017

Award-winning artist Drew Friedman's comics and illustrations have appeared in *RAW*, *Weirdo*, *Heavy Metal*, *National Lampoon*, *SPY*, *MAD*, *Time*, the *New Yorker*, the *New York Times*, the *New York Observer* and many other publications, as well as on numerous book covers. In his *New York Times* book review of *Old Jewish Comedians*, Steven Heller wrote: "A festival of drawing virtuosity and fabulous craggy faces. Drew Friedman might very well be the Vermeer of the Borscht Belt." New York's Society of Illustrators hosted a two-floor main gallery showing of all of Friedman's *Old Jewish Comedians* drawings in 2014. Filmmaker Kevin Dougherty is preparing a documentary, *Vermeer of the Borscht Belt*, covering Friedman's career.

A major exhibition of Friedman's illustrations depicting all the presidents will be held at the Billy Ireland Cartoon Library & Museum at Ohio State University in fall 2019.

Drew Friedman and his wife Kathy Bidus live in rural PA with their rescue beagle Gunther.

Thanks to the following people who helped me immensely in creating this book: My wife Kathy for all her support and for also suggesting the title of this book; Kevin Dougherty, research/fun fact consultant; Phil Felix, for lettering "Drawn to Presidents"; Kurt Andersen for his insightful and witty foreword; Jake Tapper and Patton Oswalt for their generous blurbs; John Wendler and Stephen Kroninger for their help with photo reference; my editor Eric Reynolds and book designer Keeli McCarthy at Fantagraphics Books, both the absolute best; Special thanks to Mark G. Parker.